**Praise from America's heartland
for a major autobiography!**

"Even those who have followed the radio and television ministry of Oral Roberts through the years will find new information and inspiration in this gripping narrative."
Huntsville Times

"THE CALL is a personal testament of faith and commitment in the 20th century. It is the faith of a man who has overcome many adversities to minister the message of Christ to Christians and non-Christians alike."
Asheville Citizen-Times

"Oral Roberts tells his story in a homespun manner. His is a standout example of the American rags-to-riches dream come true. The suits are first quality now, but don't be misled: the salary he receives is modest. In reading his account I found myself, all unintended."
Eternity

The Call

Oral Roberts' autobiography

AVON
PUBLISHERS OF BARD, CAMELOT, DISCUS, EQUINOX AND FLARE BOOKS

AVON BOOKS
A division of
The Hearst Corporation
959 Eighth Avenue
New York, New York 10019

First Avon Printing, January, 1973.
Fourth Printing

AVON TRADEMARK REG. U.S. PAT. OFF. AND
FOREIGN COUNTRIES, REGISTERED TRADEMARK—
MARCA REGISTRADA, HECHO EN CHICAGO, U.S.A.

Printed in the U.S.A.

CONTENTS

THE CALL

CHAPTER 1

Who's Oral Roberts?

"Oral Roberts, are you for real?" I had only met the man asking the question a few hours before and I wasn't at all sure what he meant. I told him that if he meant does Oral Roberts exist, he had only to reach out and touch me.

"No," he said, "I mean all this stuff I hear about you."

When I asked "what stuff?" I discovered he had an interesting opinion of me based on newspaper accounts, a television show of mine he had seen in the late fifties, and what he had heard people say.

Somehow meeting me in person and hearing me talk about this ministry made him question his previous opinion. Now he wanted to know if I were for real or false.

In the past twenty-five years, the name Oral Roberts has symbolized different things to different people. There have been those who have praised me to the sky, and others who have ridiculed me. But once a person was exposed to my ministry, he seldom remained indifferent. However, too many times reactions have been extreme both ways.

An example of one extreme occurred early in my ministry. A man with whom I was very close and who had been instrumental in leading me to Christ was visiting with me. We were sitting in my hotel room relaxing when he suddenly came over and knelt before me.

"Put your hands on me and pray for me."

When I asked what was wrong he reminded me of an incident that had happened only hours before in my crusade.

We were having an outstanding meeting. The tent was the biggest in the nation. Each night thousands of people from all over the Southeast packed it. All the chairs were taken at least two hours before the service began. There was an excitement in the meetings that was electrifying.

On this night I had just finished preaching, had started to go to a little cubicle right behind the platform to rest a minute and have a glass of lemonade. From there I was planning to go to the room that we designated as the "invalid room." This was for people who were so ill they could not stand in line to be prayed for. I always prayed for them first following my sermon, and then for those in the prayer line afterwards.

But before I could go to them, my friend had come running to me. He said, "Oral, come quick."

I replied, "I must go to the invalid room and pray first. Can it wait?"

"No, Oral. Come now. There is a young boy who has gone berserk. The police are holding him outside the tent. They want you to come right now and see what you can do for him."

He told me what had happened as we walked toward the boy. The boy's mother and father had brought him to the service that night to be prayed for, but in the middle of the service he had broken away and run outside the tent and begun tearing off his clothes and screaming at the top of his voice.

The policemen had seen him, had run over and caught him, and held him until his parents got there. As I approached I saw policemen on each side of a wild-looking young man with a man and woman in tears looking on.

When I came up, I asked the father about the youth. He told me he was twenty-two years old and completely uncontrollable. The parents were at the end of their rope and had come to this meeting as a last resort.

I then turned to the boy and looked straight into his eyes. I saw deep torment and fear. He had succeeded in tearing part of his clothes off, and in the struggle with the police had gotten dirt on his face and in his hair.

As I reached out my hand to place it on his head, he began to scream with rage and anger. He tried desperately to claw my hands away, but with the help of the policemen I kept my hand on his head.

I said a quiet prayer. His body was shaking like a leaf in a March wind. Suddenly he slid from under my hand and collapsed on the ground. I reached down to pick him up. He leaped straight up. I looked at him a moment and the haunted look in his eyes was gone. He was as calm and normal as could be. His father rushed between us, took the boy in his arms and began to hug him, convulsing with sobs. I turned and started to walk away.

The boy cried out, "Brother Roberts, wait."

I stopped and said, "Yes?"

"I want to go with you, Brother Roberts," he said. "Can I?"

It really touched me, but I knew his place was with his family and friends. His testimony to those who had known him before was where his greatest witness could be made.

Reluctantly, he agreed. We had a short prayer in which I asked God to use his life as a testimony to others of God's concern. And then I walked away.

That was the story my friend recounted while he knelt before me. He said, "Oral, I've never seen anything like that in my life. Pray for me to be able to do that."

Though it's gratifying to find people who believe in my ministry and calling and who affirm God's working through me, I've always had 'to underscore constantly that it is God who is the source of all healing. Men like myself are only instruments.

For I know better than anyone that Oral Roberts cannot heal anyone. I know how many I've prayed for who, when I finished praying, looked up in hurt and disappointment because nothing had happened. My failures are ever before me. They do a better job of keeping Oral Roberts humble than any self-appointed critic might.

And there have been plenty of critics. While writing this book I had my secretary check back through the files. Here is one of them from the press that illustrates the other end of the pole:

HOW SCRIPTURE SHARK
MAKES HOLY HYSTERIA
A LUCRATIVE GIMMICK

When that shameless shyster known as "Rev. Oral Roberts" takes the stage to perform, one of comic strip character Marrying Sam's most expensive weddings pales beside his performance.

The whole aim of the preacher is to arouse his audience to such a peak of excitement that like any mob the slightest word or gesture will set it into headlong action.

The fake cures, the Bible screaming, the exhortations to repent—all are only masks for the cunning mob manipulator who deftly slides in his pitch when he judges the time right.

At his meetings when he signals he's ready an assistant announces him and Roberts strides briskly through a door behind the speaker's platform carrying his Bible. An organ peals out his theme song. Roberts leads the singing, grabbing the microphone by the throat as if it were a demon.

While he delivers a supercharged message that may last two hours he is a man possessed. He plays his congregation like a symphony conductor. His voice crackles and blasts. His eyes flash and his expressive hands punctuate the words that rush from him in a torrent. The sermon blends into the altar call, the summons to sinners to come forward and be saved. Throughout, the evangelist keeps an eye on the television camera asking those at home to raise their hands, sing or pray along with the tent congregation.

Some of the sick and injured are unable to come forward and now he goes to a special tent to pray for them. When he returns, Roberts takes off his coat and seats himself in a chair in front of his congregation. Behind him are local ministers who are sponsoring his campaign. Then the parade of the sick begins and he trys to pray for each one even on nights when he doesn't have the "power."

Almost as pitiful as the deluded suckers filing up to the faith-healer are the local ministers who by their very presence admit that they have themselves failed in their ministry. The local ministers import the scripture screamers like Billy Graham and Oral Roberts in the impotent awareness that their own efforts and examples cannot arouse or inspire their congregations sufficiently. . . .

Naturally this is a reaction I have never accepted, for I know better than anyone else how many tens of thousands have been saved and healed and are still being reached through this ministry. I know, too, the integrity of this ministry and the high standard of ethics we have maintained.

I have personally laid these hands of mine on more than a million people. Through the television and radio broadcasts, the mail and printed pages, tens of millions more have been reached with the message that God is good, that He can be found at the point of human need and that He wills for all men to be made whole. I guess the scripture that sums all this up for me is III John 2, "Beloved, I wish above all things that thou mayest prosper and be in health, even as thy soul prospereth."

The real answer to the question, "Who is Oral Roberts?" is told in this book. But simply put, it's this: When I lay dying with no hope or future, I discovered God at the point of my need. A good God healed me and made me whole. And then He called me to share this witness with my generation.

CHAPTER 2

Preacher's Son

On my return from taping a television special in Japan I stopped in Honolulu for minor surgery on my sinuses. Unexpectedly, for days following the operation I suffered intense pain. Nothing seemed to help.

Evelyn, my wife, prayed; friends who were with us prayed. They were all sympathetic to my problem but nothing seemed to help. Finally I asked Evelyn to call our son Ronnie and have him pray for me. When she got him on the phone I told him that the pain was so intense that I had to have relief, and that I wanted him to pray for my healing.

Ronnie suddenly took charge. He prayed a brief but forceful prayer. I lay back on my pillow, closed my eyes, and accepted my healing. The pain gradually subsided and soon I was lost in deep sleep.

It's strange that when I had a need for healing I turned to the one of my four children who has had the most difficulty with my calling to a ministry of healing. It has not been easy for him.

One day, when Ronnie was in high school, his teacher read a very critical story from the local newspaper regarding my crusade in South Africa. It had made claims and charges that simply were not true. For some unknown reason this teacher had chosen to read the story to Ronnie's class. When she finished Ronnie rose to his feet and denied that it was true, boiling with resentment that his teacher would do such a thing. That afternoon when he came home he fell apart because of the inner turmoil, the confusion and the resentment of being embarrassed in this way.

For him and my other three children, Rebecca, Roberta, and Richard, there have been, unfortunately, other similar experiences. Each of them at some time or another has had to share the criticism and misunderstanding of my ministry. But Ronnie was growing up at a time when the controversy regarding this ministry was at its highest. He perhaps more than the others had to struggle with its stigma.

Things came to a head when he enrolled at Stanford University in Palo Alto, California. Ronnie had always been an exceptional student and had unusual ability in languages. He'd spent a year overseas as a foreign exchange student. Because of his intellectual interests and drive, he was looking forward to his time at Stanford.

But instead of being a meaningful period, it turned into a nightmare. When some of the professors learned that the son of Oral Roberts was in their class, they felt it was a mandate for them to attack not only religion in general, but divine healing in particular.

Ronnie was no more immune to this onslaught than any young person would be. He began to have deep doubts about his own faith, his understanding of the Bible, and even his belief in God. But the problem was compounded because I, his father, represented in an unusually personal way all of these beliefs.

He knew of my deep commitment to the supernatural and to God's intervention in time of human need. He knew I believed in miracles and believed the Bible as God's Word. And when his professors started attacking all of this, it began to destroy not only Ronnie's faith but also to call into question his father's ministry.

One night it reached a climax. The telephone rang and Evelyn, my wife, answered it. She said it was for me. I didn't think too much of it until I got on the line and heard a deep, almost uncontrollable sobbing and realized it was Ronnie. It was almost as if he were saying, "I wish I weren't Oral Roberts' son because then everything would be all right."

The problem was so serious that I flew to his side and spent an entire week with him. I almost lost my son but through God's help we worked through the problem. And Ronnie has retained a deep and abiding faith in God and a sensitivity to the needs of people.

Perhaps one reason I was able to reach Ronnie was because I knew some of the problems he was experiencing. I, too, had at one time gone through the deep valley of resentment, of questions and doubts. As a young teenage boy, I finally came to the place where I felt I had to leave home. I had to run away. I had to get away from it all. I wanted to get away from God. I wanted to get away from the church. I wanted to get away from my parents. I resented the direction in which my life was going. It seemed my future was planned before I was born.

We lived on a little farm in Pontotoc County, Oklahoma. Because of my mother's dedication to God, it was not unusual for her to be called on in time of great need. One day three months before I was born she received a call from a neighbor, whose child was dying of pneumonia. The doctor had said the infant would not live through the night. Crying, the parents had asked Mamma, "Would you come pray for him?"

It was a two-mile walk across the fields and Mamma was six months' pregnant. It was late in the evening. When she came to a barbed-wire fence, she separated two strands of wire, one up and one down, in order to crawl through. Her dress got caught. The wind was blowing. She was tired and alone and felt very awkward. She began to pray. She said, "Oh God, I want to make a vow. I ask you to heal my neighbor's child tonight, and when mine is born, I will give him to you."

When she came to the neighbor's house she said to the father of the sick child, "God will heal your child." She went over and put her hand on the child and prayed in the name of Christ. The child's life was spared. For Mamma, that settled the matter. The baby she was carrying would be a boy and a minister.

Shortly thereafter when I was born they named me

Granville Oral, "and let's call him Oral." She took me to church and asked the pastor to lay his hands upon me and dedicate my life to God.

The name Oral, though, was an ironic choice, for as I grew up I stuttered and stammered badly.

I didn't take my stammering seriously until my first day at school. When the teacher asked my name and all the children waited to hear me say it, a sharp fear hit me in the pit of my stomach and all I could do was work my jaws. I couldn't say, "Oral Roberts." The big laugh this got made me extremely self-conscious. I began to live inside myself and train myself to talk as little as possible.

One day a gang of boys gathered around me asking my name. I refused to tell them. They began to get rough and I started running home. Mamma saw them coming and met me at the gate. We went into the house and she pulled me up on her lap. Then she told me the story of how she had given me to God before I was born, and added, "Oral, someday you will talk without stammering. God will loosen your tongue."

Combined with being a stammerer, though, was the frustration of being a preacher's son. Both of these led to many fist fights, about half of which I lost. I can still remember going home after a fight one night with so many knots on my head that not even a soft pillow could ease the pain.

And being a Pentecostal preacher's son made it even worse. Papa had originally grown up in the Methodist Church. My grandfather had been a steward in the Methodist Church, as had his people back in Wales. One

night Mamma and Papa went to a brush arbor meeting
being held by the Pentecostals. At that service Papa and
Mamma were converted and later received the experience of the baptism with the Holy Spirit with speaking
in tongues.

Speaking in tongues was unacceptable in most denominations. Though it was unquestionably a part of the life
of the early church (Acts 2:4; 10:46; 19:6; I Corinthians
14 and others), very few church leaders at the turn of
the century felt it was a valid experience for twentieth-
century Christians. And yet many lay people, like my own
parents, were strongly moved by this phenomenon.

To an outsider listening to someone speaking in
tongues, it sounded like a foreign language fluently
spoken. Yet, many times the person speaking did not have
any idea what was being said. Although he was in full
control of his senses and speaking of his own will, he was
articulating sounds which he had never heard or learned
before.

It was a form of communication with God. He was
speaking "to God" through his spirit—the tongue was only
the vehicle. It was a release of his inner self from tensions,
inhibitions and inability to reach God through his intellect alone.

Papa began to exhort and to testify of his beliefs. Before
long he left the Methodist Church and later was ordained
a minister in the Pentecostal Holiness Church.

Papa was always even-tempered and dependable, loving and kind, but limited in ambition. When he had
pastored a church for a while and felt it was going well,
he would "retire for a while." Usually he would secure a

job or go to a distant community and conduct revivals. If he were successful, he would stay at his revivals five or six weeks, and then return home with his buggy or wagon loaded with "poundings" of food and gifts from the people for his family. If the revival was slow getting started, he would close in a week and return home, but Mamma would never allow him to rest too long. As soon as the groceries ran out she pushed him out the door to get a job or accept a church or revival appointment.

As far as food and clothing went, we would either feast or starve, be as well dressed as anyone or go barefoot far into the fall and sometimes into early winter.

We children could tell when Papa was doing well in a church by the "poundings" we received. One lady was fond of giving us plenty of milk every Monday morning until one particular Sunday Papa's sermon offended her. The next morning she sent our milk but it was "blinky."

There were many times when we were reduced almost to starvation. One time Papa went off to preach a revival in a town quite a ways off, and the people did not respond financially as he had hoped. Consequently, he was not able to send money or to come home and arrange for our care. As it came suppertime one evening Mamma called my brother Vaden and me together and said, "Boys, I want to talk to you a moment." We went out on the porch and sat down and she said, "Vaden, Oral, we don't have anything to eat tonight." Immediately Vaden began to ask why. We found out that it was because Papa had not been able to send us any money.

After a while Mamma said, "Boys, we're going to go visiting tonight for the church." So we went down the street to visit Sister Campbell, a widow who had a lot of children. We got there just as they were sitting down to eat supper. Sister Campbell, when she saw us, said, "Oh, you're just in time to have supper." But Mamma's pride was too great and she said, "Oh no. We're not hungry." (It was a good thing she didn't ask Vaden and me because we certainly would have told her we were.)

Finally about nine o'clock Mamma said that we had to go. Sister Campbell suggested we have a word of prayer, so we all knelt down to pray. Mamma began praying and thanking the Lord for being so good to us. Vaden and I kind of prayed with our eyes open thinking how empty our stomachs were and wondering how Mamma could talk about everything being so good.

While we were walking home Vaden asked Mamma why she prayed like that because it didn't seem to us that God was very good; we didn't have anything to eat. Mamma explained to us as best she could and when we got home Vaden ran up on the porch to open the door. He said, "Mamma, there's something behind the door. I can't open it."

I ran up to help him and pushed the door open and turned on the light. We looked down and there was the biggest box of groceries that any of us had ever seen. When Mamma saw it she began to rejoice just as she had at Sister Campbell's and talked about how the Lord was being so good to us.

She said, "Boys, take up the groceries and put them over here on the kitchen table." Vaden and I began to empty the box and to pull out all those good things to eat. Way down in the corner was a big country ham and sacks of potatoes and flour. Soon we had the whole table covered.

Mamma took one look, pulled an apron off the wall, put it on, got out a sharp knife, and began to slice ham, peel potatoes, and make bread. It was nearly midnight when she finally said, "Boys, it's ready!"

There on the table was a big platter of country ham, hot biscuits, and potatoes. As we ate the food just seemed to melt in our mouths, and Vaden and I then realized God was really taking care of us.

This story had a happy ending, but there was a cycle of poverty in our lives that kept gnawing away at me. As I began to approach my early teens I felt I had to get away. And so one day I simply announced to Mamma and Papa that I was going to leave home. They had the normal reactions and began to protest, and Mamma to cry and Papa to exhort and to threaten. He said, "Oral, I will send for you. I will put the police on your trail and I will bring you home."

I replied, "If you do, I will just run away again."

I had made up my mind. I was on a dead-end road, and I felt my dreams could not be realized. There was no future or hope for me as the son of a poor preacher.

As I was leaving, Mamma and Papa asked me to kneel down and let them pray with me. That was kind of hard on me. We'd had a lot of prayer all my life. In fact, when I was small I felt quite sure that Jesus lived with us because Mamma and Papa talked to Him so much.

When we had knelt down, Mamma began to pray and to ask the Lord to take care of me and told Him they were committing me into His hands. As I was getting ready to go, she made me kneel down again and with tears coursing down her cheeks, she said, "Oral, you will never be able to go farther than our prayers. We will pray and ask God to send you home, and He will."

I must admit that almost made me back out. They had appealed to the side of me that deeply respected them, their prayers and their dedicated lives. But my rebellious youth conquered. I walked out of the house and out of their lives, never really intending to return. I felt I had to get into the mainstream.

CHAPTER 3

My Brush with Death

I left home in Ada and went to Atoka, Oklahoma, and found lodging in a judge's home where I was allowed to have access to his law books. I began to study these with all the hunger of a young animal searching for food, and to dream of becoming a lawyer and being governor of Oklahoma.

To support myself I followed a demanding schedule. I served as a handyman in the judge's home, had a job in a grocery store on Saturdays, threw a paper route, and wrote a column and served as a reporter for my home-town paper, the *Ada Evening News*.

My rising time was 4 A.M. when I would build the fires. I went to bed around midnight after I'd finished the day's classes, practiced ball, thrown my paper route, written my column, and maybe even had a date. At school I carried a full load. I was an A student and loved to study. I had left home to make something of myself and I worked hard at it. I was elected president of my class and made the starting basketball team, but I began to push myself beyond what I was physically able to take.

I began to have small pains in my chest and to wake up at night in deep sweats. I tired easily. Many times after a basketball game I felt my lungs would burst. Every now and then I'd cough and spit up blood, but I thought nothing of it. I was excited by what was going on, fascinated by life, and supremely confident. I felt I had my future before me and nothing could stop me.

Then it all ended one night during a basketball game. It was the final game in the Oklahoma Seven Basketball Tournament. I had the ball and was dribbling down the court driving in for a layup as hard and fast as I could when suddenly everything began to blur before my eyes. I stumbled and collapsed on the gymnasium floor. Blood began to spurt from my mouth. I lost consciousness briefly and began hemorrhaging with every breath.

My coach, Mr. Hamilton, rushed over and soon he and others picked me up and carried me to his car and laid me on the back seat. He said, "Oral, you're going home."

As I lay there looking out at the night, it seemed the world began to fall down around me. I didn't know what was wrong but whatever it was I knew it was bad. Now I was heading back to poverty, back to a religion I had never accepted, back to my parents' discipline, and it tore me up inside.

When Mr. Hamilton got to my house, he went up to the front door and knocked. Papa came to the door and Mr. Hamilton said, "Reverend Roberts?"

My father answered, "Yes. Is something wrong?"

He said, "Reverend Roberts, I've brought your son home. Can you help me carry him in?"

When Mamma saw my coach and Papa carrying me in she screamed, "Oh God, I didn't know he would come home like this."

They put me in bed and although most Pentecostals in that day were strong on divine healing and had little to do with medical doctors, my dad was an exception. The doctors were called in and began to make their examinations. I had a terrible pain in my lungs. I would get to coughing and hemorrhaging at night so much that the wallpaper next to my bed had to be removed and new wallpaper put on.

One day my father came into my bedroom after the doctor had left and he started to say something to me. Tears began to well up in his eyes. I said, "Papa, what's wrong?"

He said, "Son, you're going to be all right."

I said, "Well, if I'm going to be all right, why are you crying?"

He said, "You're going to be all right, son."

I said, "Papa, tell me what's wrong. Why do my lungs hurt? Why do I cough up blood? Why don't I want to eat any more?"

Finally he told me. When he did, the world came crashing in on me. He said, "Oral, you have tuberculosis in both lungs."

I could not believe it, but he assured me it was true. I had tuberculosis and I was to be sent either to the state tubercular sanatorium at Talihina in the mountains of eastern Oklahoma or to a quiet place in the country.

This was 1934. In those days to have tuberculosis at age sixteen was a much greater threat than it would be today. There was no penicillin, no miracle drugs. I had had relatives who had died with tuberculosis. My oldest sister Velma had died at nineteen of pneumonia. Now suddenly death was staring me in the face.

When my brother Vaden found out he came in crying, and flung himself across the bed, asking God to let him have the tuberculosis instead of me. I finally pushed him off and reached over to a little table near the bed and picked up all the medicine. I said, "Here, Papa, take this."

Papa replied, "What do you mean, Oral?"

I said, "Papa, they can't cure tuberculosis. This medicine isn't going to do any good. I'm going to die."

Mamma came into the room and took my hand and began to talk to me. I finally stopped her and said, "Mamma, what did your daddy die of?"

She looked down and didn't answer.

I said, "Mamma, tell me. What did your daddy die of?"

Finally she answered, "Of tuberculosis."

This only confirmed my fears that I, too, was going to die. Day after day I lay there questioning and crying out at my fate. Mamma, however, was convinced that God would heal me and she urged my father to write everyone we knew to pray to and believe in God for my healing. Several times groups of these friends would come to stay with us a day or two to pray for me. It all seemed like a dream. I looked at them through eyes that didn't really see and heard through ears that didn't hear.

I talked often with my mother about my future, about

being a lawyer. She would smooth my pillow, put a hand
on me or lean over and kiss my brow and say, "We'll see,
son, we'll see."

I would look at her and remember the many times she'd
told me that someday my tongue would be released and
someday I would be a preacher. Then I would begin to
grow bitter that my lungs were bursting inside, that I was
coughing day and night, that I had fever nearly all the
time, and that when I tried to stand and walk, I was so
weak that I stumbled and fell and had to have them pick
me up and lay me back on the bed.

Papa finally accepted an appointment at a small church
in Stratford, Oklahoma, so he could be home with me
all the time. People came and went. They came to see
the preacher's son who lay dying with tuberculosis.

When Papa and the coach had put me in bed, I
weighed 160 pounds on a 6-foot 1½-inch frame. After
lying bedfast for 163 days, I was down to 120 pounds.
Friends no longer recognized me. In fact, when they came
to visit me they could hardly stand to look at me.

Food tasted like wood. Sharp pains were constantly in
my chest clear through to my shoulder blades. Night
sweats were constant and the bloody coughing was always there. I began to curse the day I was born.

I took a lot of medicines prescribed by the doctors
and several homemade remedies given by well-meaning
friends. Constant prayers were said over me, predictions
were made from time to time that the end was near. I
lived in a state of unreality except for the suffering in my
body. My mind was in a shadow and it felt as if I was
away off from normal things.

I didn't respond to my parents' entreaties to pray or to be converted. A stupor engulfed me and at last it was as if I didn't see or hear anyone. I refused to take any more medicine, saying, "If I'm going to die anyway, why take that bitter-tasting stuff." I kept wondering, "Why has this happened to me? What have I done to deserve it?"

My pastor at the Methodist Church came to visit me. I had joined the Methodist Church quite a while back even though my father was a Pentecostal Holiness minister. Most of my friends were Methodist, also. I had enjoyed my church relationship very much. But now, as my pastor started to leave, he said, "Oral, you've just got to be patient."

I had never been patient even when well, and now I certainly was not interested in patiently waiting for death. I thought, "Brother, if that's all you've got to offer, I don't want it."

I was equally repelled by my parents' religion. They and the people of the church were concerned about my dying and going to hell. They would talk to me about getting saved and going to Heaven. They found it difficult to appreciate my response: "I'm not interested in dying and going to Heaven or dying and going to hell. I'm interested in living. I want to be well."

Then one day something happened that changed my attitude. My sister, Jewell, who lived seventeen miles away had an urge to come to our house. She came into my bedroom and looked down and said, "Oral, God is going to heal you."

It was as though she had turned on a light in my soul. All at once I awakened and I became aware of Jesus.

Sermons had never reached me, the beautiful songs had never touched me. But with those seven little words, my sister identified Jesus as being part of my life, part of my future and my existence. He knew my name. He knew I existed. I was a person, a human being worth saving. I had a life worth living. And He was concerned about me.

My lungs were being torn up, I stammered and stuttered, I'd run away from home, gone my own way, but God cared. He was going to heal me and He had known about me all the time.

Not too long after this my brother Elmer came to our house. Elmer was no more religious than I was, but he had attended a tent revival where an evangelist was praying for the sick. What he had seen there had convinced him that his little brother could be helped. He borrowed a car, bought gas with the last thirty-five cents he had, and drove over to get me. He came straight into my bedroom and said, "Oral, get up. God is going to heal you."

Since I had never heard him talk about religion much, I said, "Elmer, what do you mean?"

He said, "I'm taking you to a tent meeting they're having in Ada. God is going to heal you. Now get up and let's go."

I said, "Elmer, I can't get up."

He said, "Well, then, I'll carry you."

About this time Mamma and Papa came in the room. When Elmer told them what he was doing they immediately pitched in to help. Though none of my clothes would fit me now, they put an old suit on me. They couldn't afford an ambulance so they took my mattress and put it in the backseat of the car and then carried me out.

As the little car slowly made its way to Ada, I suddenly knew God was going to heal me. It was one thing for Jesus to know it . . . I had to come into a knowing myself. The promise that my mother had made to God before I was born now became a reality for me. God spoke to my heart promising to heal me and He called me to take His healing power to my generation. His words rang clear to me: "Son, I am going to heal you and you are to take the message of my healing power to your generation."

Though I didn't have any idea what that meant, I did know that now my life was in His hands. I have never ceased to believe it.

When we arrived at the tent, they put me in a rocking chair with pillows on both sides, and when the evangelist finished preaching, they carried me up to him. He put his hands on my head and said a short prayer, "Thou foul disease! I command you in the name of Jesus Christ to come out of this boy's lungs! Loose him and let him go!"

The next thing I knew I was racing back and forth on the platform shouting at the top of my voice, "I am healed! I am healed! I am healed!"

The preacher came over and took hold of me. He led me to the microphone and said, "Son, tell the people what the Lord has done for you."

All my life I had been a stutterer. I had been scared of crowds. I would freeze on the spot. But I took the microphone from his hands and spoke to that crowd as if I had spent half of my life on a platform. My tongue was loose, and I could talk. I could breathe all the way down without burning pain and coughing and hemorrhaging. I walked up and down the platform proclaiming what Jesus of Nazareth had done for me.

Later my parents took me to the Sugg Clinic in Ada, Oklahoma. There I had my lungs fluoroscoped. Dr. Morry found them absolutely perfect. He came into my room after the fluoroscopy and said, "Son, just forget you ever had TB. Your lungs are as sound as a dollar."

From poverty, to a runaway, to deathbed, and healing—it all combined to make me a preacher. Within two months of my healing I delivered my first sermon. It was a little sermon but it was a start.

CHAPTER 4

The First Healing

When I was a young struggling pastor in the mid 1940s, I kept wrestling with a deep sense of discontent. I felt frustrated and dissatisfied in my work. It seemed to me that my ministry and the outreach of my church was making no real difference in the lives of the people of our community.

The sick, the dying, the poor, the brokenhearted, the desperate—few of these looked to the church for help. More and more I was convinced that the great bulk of our time and effort in the church was spent on ourselves—meetings for church members, prayers for church members, church for church-type people. Now and then we would reach a new family and see a new face, but they were usually related to someone already in the church.

Though I was only in my late twenties I felt I was dying on the vine. Each week began to be more and more of a struggle. How could I get up and preach about Jesus making the lame to walk, the dumb to talk, the deaf to hear, the blind to see, the leper to be cleansed, and the dead raised to life and then let it all be treated as something in the past, something irrelevant to our life and time? How could I talk about the Bible being in the NOW?

I began to be consumed with a passion either to have a ministry like Jesus or to get out of the ministry. What good did it do to tell about events that weren't happening in *this* world, in the *now?*

It all came to a head in early 1947. I was then pastoring the Pentecostal Holiness Church in Enid, Oklahoma. Married with two children, I had been preaching for twelve years, but I was getting ready to find another vocation and another means to support my family rather than continue a ministry that was becoming increasingly invalid. It was not meeting the needs of people.

While pastoring I was also attending Phillips University in Enid. One day in a sociology class a comment was made by the professor that to me seemed highly inappropriate and critical of the Bible. It was the impetus I needed. From within me God spoke to my heart and said, "Don't be like others, be like Jesus."

Though class was not over, I got up and left. I went home determined either to be like Jesus or to forget the whole thing. I could not be a halfway Christian preacher.

But what was Jesus like? I went to the Bible. For many days I read the Gospels and the book of Acts on my knees. Over and over I concentrated on one man—Jesus.

I began to see that He did not come with a life-shortening suggestion, but rather with a lifesaving power.

He came against sin, disease, and fear. He was a man of compassion, of action and power.

He said, "The Spirit of the Lord is upon me, because he hath anointed me to preach the gospel to the poor; he hath sent me to heal the brokenhearted, to preach deliverance to the captives, and recovering of sight to the blind, to set at liberty them that are bruised, To preach the acceptable year of the Lord" (Luke 4:18-19).

It became clear to me that there was a great difference between being a Christian and being a follower of Jesus. A Christian is a person who at one time or another has confessed the Lordship of Jesus Christ. He may go to church, even work in the organization of the church. But being a Christian does not necessarily mean he will do what Jesus did or strive to repeat the acts of Jesus. It is necessary that he go on and become a *disciple* or a *follower*.

For me, becoming a follower of Jesus was crucial. In the book of Acts, the disciples—the followers of Jesus—kept Jesus alive in their hearts and actions. They preached, they prayed, and healings and miracles were wrought as thousands were won to Christ. These events were commonplace in the Early Church of the first century.

But they were not commonplace in America in 1947, and specifically not in the church which Oral Roberts pastored in Enid, Oklahoma. I kept comparing my ministry and my church with that of the disciples and the Early Church. They had preached in the marketplace and in the arena of need. I was preaching three times a week in my little church to the same people. The disciples ministered to the sick wherever they found them and miracles happened. The sick, the crippled, the afflicted seldom darkened the door of our church and little happened when they did.

We were not really tuned in to believing that if God existed for anyone in any age, He existed for everyone in every age. The healing Jesus was for another time and place.

I began to fast and pray. When it came time for a meal, I would figure the amount of time it normally would have taken to eat. And instead of eating I would spend the time praying.

I began to have a dream night after night in which I kept seeing the whole human race crying out to God for healing. I had never walked in my sleep before, but now several times I would awaken on my knees in another room, weeping and crying to God.

The dream was always the same: millions of people crying out for healing and help. They were waiting for a word of hope that would help them release their faith to find solace for their pain, food for their bodies, healing for their heartache, health for their bodies, and peace for their souls.

Soon I had lost over thirty pounds. Things were getting critical. Though I kept my fast a secret, people began to be concerned for my health because of my loss of weight. Yet I kept it up until suddenly, one week, the Bible began to come alive. A Biblical foundation emerged for my faith. I saw that God was good, that it was His will to heal and make whole, and that He was the source of abundant life. He spoke to me and left me without any doubt that He had called me to take His healing power to my generation. I was ready to take the steps to enter world evangelism through a ministry of healing.

Though I was ready, before I could change the whole course of my existence I had to see my decision demonstrated and validated.

I went downtown and rented an auditorium from the city. Then I prayed and told God if He had really called me, at least a thousand people would be present. And when they were, an offering would be taken quietly and simply which would pay the costs of renting the building. Finally, I said, "Lord, I'm going to do this first. I'm trusting in you. I'm expecting a miracle. If you're really in this, then heal enough people not only for me to know, but for the people to know also."

For me this was do or die. I told my church the tests I had put before the Lord. If they failed, I announced, I would be leaving the ministry. I even went down to a local clothing store and inquired whether they had an opening for a salesman who might start work that next Monday. They said they did and I said, "Good, I may be back to see you."

My reasoning was audacious and impractical. Seldom had more than two hundred attended my services at the church. To think it would increase now fivefold was ludicrous.

Money was in short supply and the rent of the auditorium for one afternoon only had been $160—a whole month's salary.

But those were really secondary considerations. What I was really concerned about was, would the people release their faith to believe God for healing? Would God use me as an instrument to bring healing to the people?

On the appointed Sunday my regular morning worship service in my church was like a funeral. I had taken a step of no return. That night I would either have entered a ministry of healing or become a haberdasher!

When the time came for the special afternoon service I rode downtown with considerable misgiving. A chain of events that began before I was born when my mother had promised me to God was now being tested. Had I really heard God call me to this ministry at age seventeen when I was being taken to a tent meeting to be prayed for? Were the past few months of intense agonizing for this purpose?

However, I had made the commitment of my life and there was no way but forward.

When I arrived at the auditorium I went to a side entrance.

The custodian was there. Somehow or other he had heard about my three tests.

He said, "Preacher, I hear you want at least one thousand people."

I said, "That's right."

"Well, I've counted them," he said.

I could wait no longer. I said, "Man, how many are there?"

"Right now there are twelve hundred seated in the auditorium!" He beamed as he reported it.

Something leaped within. *One down, and two to go.*

When it came time in the service to take the offering, I

had determined that there would be no big pull. The ushers came forward, the plates were passed. I instructed them to count the money and bring me the results.

In a few minutes a man brought a slip of paper with the amount written on it. When I looked at it, it said $163.03— $3.03 more than was needed. *Two down, but now came the only real test*—meeting the needs of the people.

I preached a sermon entitled, "If you need healing, do these things." In the middle of my sermon I jumped off the platform onto the main floor. Although I had not finished preaching, the people started toward me.

An old German woman with a withered hand was one of the first to reach me. I grabbed her hand and prayed, "In the name of Jesus Christ of Nazareth be healed!"

Her arm shot up in the air, she screamed and began opening and closing her hand.

It electrified the whole house. Seven men left their chairs, came to the front, and knelt down asking God to save them.

A line of sick people formed to my right and I began praying for people with all forms of disease and sickness. Healing after healing occurred.

Finally, at six o'clock, the last person had been prayed for. I started for the back door. Every stitch of my clothing was wringing wet. I was exhausted physically, but strong as a lion inside.

Not everyone had been healed, but a sufficient number had been helped to let me and the people know that God had used me as His instrument to bring healing to the people.

I had entered a ministry that would one day take me
to all continents and most of the nations of the world.
Through radio, television, and film we would go into tens
of millions of homes. Offices would be established in six
foreign countries. We would send out over 100 million
printed pieces a year, and these would be translated into
more than 163 languages. An international office would
be established in Tulsa employing over six hundred people. A multimillion-dollar university would be built that
would perpetuate this ministry for generations to come.

It was all decided by the $163.03 given by the twelve
hundred people who came to that service, but more than
that, by the God of Heaven who chose to raise up a ministry to recapture for the church the healing Jesus.

CHAPTER 5

Success and Failure

In 1947 before entering this ministry I was awakened night after night in the midst of a dream in which the human race was passing by me sick and wanting healing. The dream was always the same. In it I saw man as he is lost from God, tormented, going to and fro in an endless quest for healing and life. Seeing this in a dream is one thing; experiencing it face to face with the people is another! After twenty-five years of being in the arena with suffering people, I know that what I experienced in 1947 was more than a dream.

In one of our crusades one afternoon I laid my hands on more than nine thousand sick people and prayed for each one individually to be healed! More than nine thousand in a space of three hours. When it was over I nearly collapsed. My body felt in a state of shock. My eyes wouldn't focus normally and my hands shook. My right arm and shoulder seemed numb except for a dull ache near the shoulder blade. When I tried to eat, the food wouldn't go down. When I lay down, my body jerked all over. Sleep was out of the question for hours, and when I slept it was for only an hour or two at a time.

The next morning my legs would barely move and my flesh was sore from head to toe. My body took five days to relax and recover strength.

During this time my mind was racing. It simply would not settle down. Thoughts of all those people flooded my mind. I could see them one by one, vividly recalling things about them, and hearing what they said to me. Those nine thousand were like the whole human race stretching endlessly around the world, all moving toward me, each crying out his need. My dream was relived.

A woman with an afflicted child and of a religious persuasion that does not accept miracles was present at one service. When I had finished and was on the way to my room, she had become about half persuaded there was something to it after all. Not wanting to join the group publicly, she called to me as I was leaving. She could not know how I felt in every bone. When I suggested she bring the child the next day when I would be fresh in strength again, she exploded and spit in my face, calling me names I won't repeat and screaming, "You fraud." A team member took me by the arm and led me to the car while she continued to curse me.

I should not have allowed this to hurt me. Perhaps I was selfish. I kept saying, "Doesn't she understand that it is God's healing power and not me that heals. Doesn't she realize that when one's physical strength goes he is unable to minister until he rests? Doesn't she know?"

All this was futile, of course, for how could she understand? She had been taught by her religion that the days of miracles were past. Even when she had witnessed actual healings and felt her heart softening a bit, she still clung to her reservations. Thrusting her child at me and saying, "Heal my child," and hearing me reply, "Not now, bring him back when I am rested," she was unable to control her emotions.

I did, though, reach a place where I no longer wanted to pray for sick people. It happened several years ago during one of our largest crusades.

I had preached on this particular evening with unusual freedom; a large number had responded to the invitation to accept Christ. Then, as was my custom, I went immediately to the invalid room where the most serious cases were waiting. It had always been my custom to pray first for those who could not stand before the public line. These people were so sick they could not go through a prayer line, and it was necessary for me to come to them. Many times at the start of the service I would go through the invalid room before preaching so that when I delivered my sermon, I would have a focus on people in need.

This particular night when I went into the invalid room the first man I approached was dying of cancer. That in itself was not unusual, for I had prayed for thousands of people who had this terrible disease—and many of them had testified to a touch of healing from the Lord. But as I came to this man to reach out my hands to pray, the odor of dying flesh hit me in the face. I caught my breath, my stomach began to churn, and I wheeled around and began to run for the door.

Outside I retched until my stomach seemed as if it would turn inside out. For a moment, I wanted to be anywhere, do anything but go back in and face that man. I tried to summon up my courage. I thought of the man and the rejection and pain he must be feeling. I thought of the many other people present in that room who had seen me refuse to pray. I thought of my team, and the hundreds inside waiting for prayer.

But nothing helped. I didn't want to pray for that man— and that man represented tens of thousands of others who wanted to hear a word of faith, who needed to know that Jesus cared and that there were Christians willing to identify with them in their need, yes, even to touch them and pray for them. From within me I heard God saying, "If you don't go back in there and pray for that man, you're not worthy to be called a Christian." It shook me.

Quietly I began praying to Jesus. And as I prayed a calmness began to come over me. Strength began to flow through me, and suddenly, as if by divine insight, I realized that Oral Roberts was not being called upon to heal that man, but to pray for him. My responsibility was to take Jesus to him and through prayer and the laying on of hands to believe with him for healing to begin.

I walked to that same man's side with a smile on my face and compassion beating in my heart and said, "Brother, in the name of Jesus Christ of Nazareth, be healed."

He smiled back; then tears began to form in his eyes. He slowly rose up and made his move toward deliverance. I went to others in the room and as I touched them, I felt divine anointing and help being released.

I've often wished I had followed up on that man to see how God continued working in his life. But I know this. Through that man's need, Jesus of Nazareth ministered to me in a way that profoundly influenced me. A momentary weakness was turned into strength and a resolve to pray for people in need which I've never lost.

Once while at home I made an emergency call upon a boy in the hospital who had been critically injured and was not expected to live through the day. While his doctor stood by, I prayed for him. He was not healed. In spite of the doctor's treatment and my prayers, he died the next day. Because of this failure, I was asked, "Why are some healed and some are not?"

I replied, "I don't know all the answers, but I do know that not even when Christ was here was everyone healed."

This is a shocker. People usually think that Christ never failed when He prayed for the sick. But that's contrary to the Bible, for it states very clearly in Mark 6:5 that He left Nazareth because of the people's unbelief and because He could do no mighty miracles there. It does not say He did not; it says He could not. Not even He could heal or bring about a miracle where the conditions were not right.

If I felt that I alone were responsible for healing, I doubt if I could retain my sanity, for no man can continually confront the sick and the dying without sensing the desperation and the pleading for help.

I've had a lot of physicians talk to me about the traumas they have experienced when they are constantly confronted by the intensely ill. When they have lost a patient on the operating table, several have told me that it has taken them days to get over it. Ministering to people through prayer could be equally as destructive were it not for God's help.

When an associate of mine joined our editorial staff a few years ago, his first assignment was to report the Columbus, Ohio, crusade for *Abundant Life* magazine. This man had been raised in a home where they prayed for the sick. He had prayed for the sick himself when pastoring and had been acquainted with my ministry for several years.

Following my sermon the first night of the Columbus crusade, he joined me to go to the invalid room to pray. Later he told me about it. "I wasn't ready," he said. "I had never seen that many people dying in one room together. There were living skeletons lying on cots with the most desperate look in their eyes I had ever seen. Babies with huge heads, families hovering over their sick relatives. A lot of them were old—but many were very young.

"I remember two especially. One was a young man in a wheelchair. He must have been at least six and a half feet tall, for he dwarfed the chair. The parents told you of a sporting accident their son had been in which had left him an invalid. I immediately recognized the name and remembered the newspaper account. As I looked at him and then at his mother and father, it really tore me up. You prayed. The parents prayed. Everything was said that could be said. Yet he was not healed.

"The other person was outside the invalid tent. After you had started back to the main tent, I noticed a young girl over by the tent, lying on the ground sobbing and groaning as if she were seriously hurt. I went over to her and asked if I could be of assistance.

"When she finally gained control of herself, I saw she was just a young girl in her teens. When I asked what was wrong she said, 'My mother is in there,' pointing to the invalid tent.

"I said, 'I see.'

"She said, 'No you don't. She's dying and if God doesn't heal her, I don't think I can live. What can I do?'

"I couldn't answer that question. I went slowly back into the main tent.

"Later my leg began to itch. When I raised my pants leg, I looked and a big nerve welt had risen.

"My question is, 'Oral, how do you take it? What do you say to people who aren't healed?'"

That's not an easy question, and I've never been able to answer it completely.

Not too long ago I appeared on the David Frost TV show and Barbara Walters from the "Today" show was also a guest. She asked the same question, only a little differently.

"If it's God's will to heal, why isn't everyone healed?"

This is a question I had to wrestle with very seriously when I first began my ministry. "What if I pray for someone and he doesn't receive any help? What if *I* fail?"

As I prayed over this, the Lord spoke to me and told

me that if I were to decide my future on whether or not I would ever fail, then I would never have a ministry.

I have failed many times. There have been instances when two people were in the prayer line together with the same affliction. One would receive help; the other would not. I've never understood it. I know if Oral Roberts were the healer, I would empty the hospitals.

In fact, for years in our crusades local congregations of the Churches of Christ in that city would take full-page ads in the newspapers attacking my ministry and challenging me to a debate. One of their most repeated ploys was usually, "If Oral Roberts can heal, why doesn't he empty the hospitals?"

Though they felt their cause was just, I never was led to respond to them. And when Church of Christ people came through the prayer line, I always did my best to let them know of my interest in them and desire to see them healed. Ironically, some of our closest friends and partners are from the Church of Christ.

I have been asked, "Is unbelief always the cause of failure?"

My reply is that there are many things about healing we do not know. In my brief experience I have prayed for some people with all the faith that I possessed and the person was not healed. In other instances, my faith was not as strong as I thought it should be and still the person was healed. I don't know how to explain that except to say there is only One who knows what is inside you or me and what it takes to really bring about a miracle. A doctor works with all the skill and compassion and faith at his command; some he helps, some he does not. It is the same way with prayer. Just as you have to draw strength from those you help and refuse to be discouraged when you fail, so must we continue our work in the face of both success and failure.

There's no way to make praying for the sick easy. If the people who come only had minor afflictions—headaches, hay fever, or a cold—there would be no great risk.

But when you say, "I believe God heals," and you're willing to be an instrument of God for healings, then you have to risk facing the worst possible cases—and failures. And we've even had three people die during our crusades.

You can't have over a million people a year in the crusades without somebody dying. I admit that through the years when I allowed myself to think about it, it was a shaking experience. For if you get ten thousand people together, many of them seriously ill, what if fifteen people died while you were praying for them? In any normal circumstances at least fifteen would die. But I've never felt the atmosphere of our crusades is ordinary. Someone else is there.

Once during our crusade in Detroit, Michigan, I woke up one morning and was reading the Detroit *Free Press* and discovered that a woman who had attended our crusade the night before had died.

Immediately, I checked with my associates and discovered the story was true. The woman, a diabetic, had attended our crusade. I didn't remember praying for her specifically, but she had gone to one of my associates and told him that she had been healed. She wanted to testify to the entire crusade audience.

When I learned of it, I refused to let her. I told my associate to tell her about our procedures for testimonies, namely, that we never permitted testimonies of immediate healings, only those that had been verified.

Several people had already testified at this crusade who had attended other crusades some time back. Their testimonies had stood the test of time, and had been verified by our office staff in Tulsa.

I had no particular feeling that this woman had or had not experienced a significant improvement, yet it was not for me to determine. That was a physician's responsibility.

Undaunted, the woman continued to proclaim her healing and decided not to continue her insulin shots. She died as a result.

I must admit that the newspaper carried a fairly accurate account of the incident based on the information they had available. But when a large weekly magazine sent its reporter, it was an entirely different matter. When they approached my associate evangelist, Robert F. De-Weese, because of his previous encounters with them he didn't expect a fair report and told the reporter so. In fact, he offered personally to buy her the biggest steak in Texas if she were only halfway fair and accurate. Sadly enough, he didn't have to.

The story castigated our ministry. There was nothing to do but bear it.

People die every day in our large hospitals, yet physicians who dedicate their lives to healing the sick are not

held up to riducule because they are not always successful.

I prayed for an Indian man in Calgary, Alberta, Canada, who was 102 years of age. He had never accepted
Christ before but was saved that night. I prayed for God
to give him strength according to his years. During the
crusade he died. This was reported in the press in a manner that put the crusade in a bad light. That evening I
stated publicly, "I am glad that this man came to our crusade. It was here that he found Christ for the first time.
It is true that his life was not extended and he has gone
to be with the Lord. However, I am proud that we had a
chance to minister to him."

While in a crusade in Johannesburg, South Africa, I
traveled with the sponsoring pastors to a colony of lepers
where hundreds were waiting to die with this ancient
affliction (also known as Hansen's disease).

I've never forgotten that day. I saw men and women
with their bodies partially eaten away. Where a hand
used to be, there was only a stub. Part of a face was gone.
One man had lost a foot. It broke me up.

The thought came, "If you lay hands on these people,
you might catch leprosy. Then what will become of your
ministry?"

At first I felt like cringing. Then I felt like running away
and saying, "What does all this have to do with me?" But
I could not run. Healing is not something that I can take
or leave. I cannot be neutral about it. It reached me in the
extremity of my young life and through it Christ delivered
me. Squaring my shoulders, I walked toward the lepers
and began to lay hands upon them and pray in the name

of Jesus Christ. Some stood stolid and unmoving. It was difficult to tell if they were responding or not. Others received my prayers as if I were an angel sent from God, their faces lighting up in smiles and words of praise to God flowing from their lips.

I preached and prayed for hundreds that day. It was an experience that tendered my heart. I do not know how much good was done; I do know much good was done inside me.

When healing comes, it is not simply because someone has a need. To me, the ultimate purpose of healing is to bring the person into a closer relationship to God and man. Healing is not an end in itself but a means to an end—to be a better person and to do good in the world in which we live.

CHAPTER 6

Accused

I've never been arrested or in jail, but I've almost been. In the early 1960s in a crusade in Miami, Florida, the atheist association of this nation set out to humiliate me personally and embarrass this ministry and its friends by having me put in jail.

The charge they trumped up was "practicing medicine without a license." They intended to close down the crusade.

The leader of the effort was a local attorney in Miami and an outspoken atheist, who had been bragging for a long time that he would put Oral Roberts in jail.

In fact, when another evangelist had come to Florida for services, this attorney *had* succeeded in putting him in jail. The charge—"practicing medicine without a license."

His success then had made him feel confident that he could do the same with me, and I must admit I did not take his threat lightly.

During the crusades before I prayed for the people I always told them that Oral Roberts could heal no one. If they received any help, it would be because God had helped them. I was only an instrument. After I had prayed for a person, if he or I felt something had happened, I never told him he was healed. I would say, "I believe something has happened to you tonight. Go home to your doctor and find out." If God had really done something, it would stand the test of any physician.

Yet even though this was my practice, I knew that with thousands coming before me it would be a very easy thing to plant someone in the prayer line and trump up false charges. When I came to Miami for the crusade, one of the local newspapers had already been contacted by the atheist attorney and a big story had appeared pitting him against me. The atheist was quite confident that he would be successful and that in a very short time Oral Roberts would be behind bars.

Since I knew this was no idle threat, we contacted an attorney for legal advice. He assured us that as long as we held our typical services of singing, preaching, and praying we were safe, but that we would have to be on our guard, for the man could very well be planning to plant a hoax and use this to "expose us."

After we came from the lawyer's office and met with our crusade staff to brief them, I felt we had done all that was humanly possible. It was then I knew I must pray.

Praying then may sound strange but it's always been my custom. I've never felt that God's miracle power was for the purpose of making things easy for us or to cause us not to be diligent and industrious.

As an example, not too long ago I had a very seriously abscessed tooth. I went to my dentist in Tulsa and he worked on it, but it continued to bother me. Finally I went to him again.

He said, "I just don't know what to do with this."

I asked, "Do you mean by that you don't know anything else to do?"

He replied, "I'm afraid so, Oral."

I said, "Okay, I know what to do now."

As long as I knew there was medical help I really had little faith for healing. But when I knew there was no medical help, my faith became stronger. I went home and talked to the Lord and prayed for myself. The following day I felt there was a change in my mouth and I returned to him.

He examined me and said, "Oral, have you been to another dentist?"

I said, "No."

He said, "This is amazing. You're okay. What did you do?"

I said, "Well, when you told me that you could do no more, I found I could use my faith. I used both medical and spiritual healing."

He said, "Well, I can't approve or disapprove of spiritual healing, but I can tell you this is my first experience with it and I'm impressed."

And the same principle held with the threat of this atheist. I had done all that could be done and yet I knew that it could very well not be enough. I knew God would have to help.

So there in Miami I began to pray, and as I prayed I

thought of the beginning of this ministry and the commitment I had made. It had been a long time since that first meeting in Enid in 1947. I had preached to tens of millions of people all over the world through our crusades and television and personally prayed for a comparable number in the same way.

Now an atheist was trying to discredit it all. The Lord began to speak to me and to give me courage and faith. My fear began to leave. I got to my feet and felt ready and able whatever might happen. The confidence that I received from God was that I did not need to fear going to jail because it would not hurt my ministry. He assured me that it was strong and solid enough to withstand such an assault.

I knew that the success of this ministry was not dependent upon my ability or my efforts. I'd always felt a calling from God and a divine urgency that was from Him.

Now at the crusade instead of being concerned about my every word, I felt a holy freedom. As a former stutterer and stammerer, I knew what fear of saying the wrong things could do. God's reassurance to me at this hour was one of the high points of my ministry.

The very first night of the crusade I began preaching like a new man. I ceased trying to say the right words for an atheist, a lawyer, and a sinner. Instead, I sought to say the words that would reach people in need, atheists included.

In the prayer line I felt a strength I hadn't had for years. I was eager to pray for people and their needs. The crusade team later told me they had not heard me preach with such intensity and effectiveness in some time. The atheist made his effort but the threatened jailing never came off. The crusade was a great success and hundreds were helped. There was no cause for charging me with practicing medicine without a license.

Sometimes physicians have even brought their patients in the prayer line. One night in our crusade in Trenton, New Jersey, I was preparing to pray for a woman with a goiter. Right next to her was a physician who had brought eight of his patients. As he came up, Bob DeWeese told me who he was and I reached over and shook his hand.

I then prayed for the woman with the goiter. She received her healing and I turned to him and I said, "As a physician what do you think of that?" He put his hand on her neck and saw that it was gone. He said, "Reverend Roberts, all I can ask is, where did the goiter go?"

I was astonished at his question. I replied, "Doctor, I don't know where it went. All I want to know, is it gone?"

He smiled and said, "It's gone."

He said, "I have eight or nine of my patients with me here in the line. Some of these have been helped. Others apparently not. All of them believe in your ministry. They all wanted to come and asked me to come with them. I'm not an unbeliever. I know the power of faith. Would you please lay your hands upon them and pray?"

It was a great privilege for me. Too, it was a testimony to the audience to see a well-known surgeon and a minister of the Gospel side by side. I prayed audibly. He prayed silently. But we both prayed to the same healing Christ.

After the service he talked with me at length. Later I

learned that he wrote a letter to the medical society in Columbus, Ohio, where my next crusade was scheduled, urging the physicians to try and understand this ministry. He wrote that he was convinced my work was not against physicians and that he felt the doctors should better understand the healing power of prayer.

Regrettably, though, one severe misunderstanding that has plagued this ministry and other ministries concerned with more than the spiritual needs of man is the tendency to separate divine healing from natural healing—to say either God alone can heal or that physicians alone can heal.

The result is that some people feel they're being less than faithful if they go to a physician instead of trusting solely in God, or even that taking medicine is a lack of faith.

One of my associates was raised in a family where this happened. His brother was seriously ill and their parents, both godly people, kept an around-the-clock prayer vigil. A friend of the family who had some practical nursing experience came to see them. When she saw the small infant she told them he was about to die and urged them to get medical help. Finally they relented. The doctor came and did all he could, but it was not enough. The child died. The physician later told the family, "If I had only been called sooner the child could have been saved."

Fortunately, I was raised in a home that believed all healing comes from God. The ability a physician has is God-given ability. The medicine he administers is part of God's creation.

The Bible says, "Every good gift and every perfect gift is from above, and cometh down from the Father of lights . . ." (James 1:17).

Above all authority on this earth is divine authority. That does not minimize doctors and medicine; rather, it subordinates all power to divine power.

All healing is from God. When a person receives healing through medical science or through the power of faith he should give the glory to God.

When I was dying of tuberculosis I was under the treatment of three physicians. While under their treatment I was taken to a religious service and prayed for. I experienced a marvelous transformation at that time. From that day forward I began to improve and was completely healed.

But I have never said the medicine and care given by the physicians was not helpful. I might have died had it not been for them. However, it was prayer added to their efforts that caused me to get well. For that, to God be the glory.

In 1968 I made a decision which caused quite a ripple in the church world. I rejoined the Methodist Church. I'll tell more about this in another chapter, but one thing especially relates to this matter of medicine and healing by faith.

On the weekend before I was supposed to go before the Oklahoma Annual Conference of the United Methodist Church for transfer of my ordination to the Methodist Church I became seriously ill. Talk about pain!

I have a very low threshold for pain anyway and this was excruciating. In addition to the publicity which would attend my being sick and unable to appear for the ordination (*Time* magazine, Associated Press, UPI, and others were all there), it was also commencement week at Oral Roberts University. A full round of activities was planned.

Then our campus physician came and made a preliminary examination. He said, "Kidney stones." Tests were made and a specialist confirmed his diagnosis.

Our Prayer Group was praying and my associates were praying. In fact, my wife had everyone she knew praying for my healing.

I know the prayers helped, but my physician was instrumental, too, from a nonmedical point of view. He's a fine Methodist layman and after he had given me a shot to relieve the pain, he said, "Oral, now I want to pray for you."

That was some feeling. I had known a lot of doctors but he was a rare one. He laid his hands on me and said a very quiet, short prayer and then left.

I went to sleep and slept for four hours. In the meantime, the doctor told Evelyn that if I was no better when I awoke, he had made arrangements to send me to the hospital for surgery. But something happened while I slept, for when I awoke the pain was gone. X rays later showed that a stone had passed.

Was it the doctor and his medicine or the doctor and his prayer? I just know I was able to be up and around. And I was able to keep every appointment that week!

One of the books that has impressed me as much as any I know is *The Doctors Mayo* which is about the famous Mayo surgeons of the Mayo Clinic in Rochester, Minnesota. While reading their biography, I was inspired by two things—one, their absolute dedication to the relieving of human suffering; second, they saw that they had to operate. At that time, around 1900, surgery had not become a major factor in the practice of medicine. And these men, the father and two sons, undertook a new type of surgery. As I recall, appendicitis was the major part of their effort. A lot of people died—apparently a larger percentage than was to be expected.

They were vilified, they were misrepresented, they were called "butchers," but they knew they had something. They knew there were certain conditions in the human body that could be corrected only through surgery.

And they dedicated themselves to surgery. They used St. Mary's Hospital as their place of work, and as a result thousands and thousands of people began to think of Rochester and the Mayo brothers as the number-one place for medical help in the world.

Now they are more than famous. But in those early days they were highly controversial. Most of the organized medical fraternities spoke out against them, but they quietly went about their work anyway. They did not reply to their critics. When they made speeches over the nation they told of those who had died and those who had lived. And it was the Mayo brothers who turned the medical world around.

When I read that, it struck a part of me because as a

young evangelist starting out I knew I had something. I knew that religion must be focused upon the individual. We must not get carried away with the practice of religion as an end in itself. I knew that religion had to focus upon and zero in on the actual needs of the human being. What I was attempting to do, I felt, was tantamount to medical surgery. I identified, as the Mayo brothers did, with the people who had the worst needs. With many of these people I failed. It was obvious.

But I began to publish stories in *Abundant Life* magazine of those whom I had helped through God's power and also began to put them on television. Gradually we broke down a lot of opposition. Even people who never noticed me accepted the possibility of healing. As a result there was a noticeable change toward healing in the whole church world.

Another physician who made a deep impression on me was Dr. Christiaan Barnard. Barnard was a young man, very much like the Mayo brothers in that he, too, had a deep insight into human beings. He came to America, where he trained at the University of Minnesota under the greatest heart man of that time. Barnard was not afraid to attempt new techniques in heart operations and secretly had in his mind the idea that someday he would transplant a heart.

South Africa was probably one of the few places on the earth where he could do this. He could not possibly have performed the first heart transplant in America because of the laws which prohibited it, but in South Africa this was not the case. Too, Dr. Barnard had a fanatical dedication to his goal. Everybody who has ever done anything has had this dedication. He would not be deterred. He was willing to take a risk, and I was inspired by that.

Another thing I have learned from doctors is that they usually seem very aloof and cold in their approach. They have learned that when they become sympathetic they are no longer able to help the person. No matter what they feel within them toward the patient, they try to remain a little distant.

When I'm praying for people or walk through a room of very ill people, my first reaction is sympathy. The whole thing is a shock to my system. I think, "This could be me. This could be a member of my family." I recall when I was ill and lay in bed so long.

I feel sympathy. I'm utterly helpless because it's not a feeling that causes me to want to pray or a feeling that makes me want to help them get rid of their afflictions. It's just that I'm so sorry. I feel so sorry for them. I feel pity.

Then I have to get away from the feeling of sympathy and look upon them as Jesus did. The Bible says when He saw the sick He was moved with compassion (Matthew 14:14). Then I begin to see people as individuals. I see the forces attacking their beings, reducing them to nothing. At that time I begin to experience a feeling within myself of the love of Christ. It is so strong it's almost like hatred. Suddenly I have hatred for the powers that have fastened upon the minds and bodies of these people and I have an almost irresistible urge to touch them and to rid them. It's a fierceness that possesses me.

People say when they look at me I look like I'm mad. My eyes are blazing. I'm not smiling. They say I look holes through them. I come up and look at them and I'm locked in with them. I look right through them. I'm totally unaware of the way I look, but some people, I've learned, wonder about this. This is compassion and when compassion hits me it rids me of sympathy. It identifies me with the person. It gives me an urge to touch him in Christ's name and see him relieved of his sickness.

Many things contribute to the healing process. A look, a word, a communication of spirit helps. Surgical skill, medication, nursing care, play their part. And it is absolutely amazing what prayer can do when offered in a positive manner for a person who cooperates by releasing his faith at the same time. Miracles can and do happen. For this we need no license except compassion for people and faith to believe.

One of the outstanding miracles of my ministry happened in a crusade in Roanoke, Virginia, in the early fifties. It was so miraculous that *Look* magazine reported it. The crowds in the American Legion Hall were unbelievably large. Thousands were turned away, for fire marshals had refused to let any more in. Even the crusade organist was unable to get inside one night.

As the service was closing, a ten-year-old child named Willie somehow managed to get into the invalid room. He didn't know that I had already prayed for the invalids and in fact was leaving the auditorium to head for home following this last service.

As I passed by the room where the invalids had been, my eye caught the picture of a little boy sitting in a chair by himself with his crutches under his arm. Despite my exhaustion, I turned and went in.

I said to him, "Son, what's your name?"

He answered, "Willie."

"Willie," I asked, "what are you doing in here?"

He said, "I'm waiting on Oral Roberts. I'm supposed to be healed today."

I looked at him a moment and then said, "Willie, I'm Oral Roberts. But when Brother Roberts is tired, his faith is not very strong."

With the honesty that only a ten-year-old can have, he said, "I don't know about that, but I'm supposed to be healed today."

Reluctantly, I said, "Willie, Brother Roberts is going to put his hands on you and pray. And I'm going to ask Jesus to heal you, but you're going to have to pray and believe with me. Okay?"

He nodded. I said a short prayer, patted him on the shoulder, and said good-bye.

I learned later what happened when he got home. He took off his braces, laid his crutches down, and said, "Momma, I'm going to walk . . ." and walk he did!

"The next day," as Willie told us later, "I couldn't go to school on Monday morning because I didn't have any shoes that would fit me. The built-up shoe was useless because both legs were now the same length. So my mother had to take me downtown in Lynchburg to buy me some normal shoes before I could go to school.

"It was late when I arrived at school that day. And when I walked into the classroom, it almost broke up the school. My classmates had never seen me except on crutches.

"Everybody shouted and the teacher cried. Then she asked lots of questions. She asked me what had happened, and I told her that I had been to Roanoke where a preacher prayed for me, and that I was healed. The teacher asked me how much he charged, and I told her, 'He didn't charge a penny.'"

When Willie was eighteen, we checked on him again. From Willie and his parents the full story came out:

When Willie was seven he developed a limp in his right leg. The leg shrank until it was a full two and a quarter inches shorter than the left one. The doctors diagnosed it as Perthes' disease. They said that nothing could be done for it, and for four years Willie walked on crutches and a built-up, corrective shoe.

Three times a day, for an hour each time, Willie had to be bathed in hot salt water. When this did not bring any improvement, he was taken to the hospital and remained three weeks with a ten-pound weight attached to his leg. But this also failed to bring relief, and he was placed in a heavy, cumbersome cast up to his shoulders.

Finally, all hope was gone. The doctor told his mother, "You must realize that this is not unusual. Nine out of ten people who have this disease never walk again."

It was, indeed, a trying and discouraging experience. And when they came to my crusade in Roanoke the first two times they could not get in because of the crowd.

The third time, as they were waiting outside the American Legion Hall, it began to snow. As they waited in the cold and snow, Willie's mother prayed. She felt in her heart that now was God's time to heal her son.

Finally, Willie managed to get in. And the rest is history.

CHAPTER 7

Violence Stopped Me

I had never seen the man before. Why he fired the gun, I'll never know. In fact, in court he himself said he did not know why he had tried to kill me. Yet a few inches were the difference between life and death.

It happened while I was holding my first meeting after leaving the pastorate in Enid. A close friend, Steve Pringle, had a tent up in Tulsa and had been holding services with different evangelists for several weeks. When he learned I was in town, he invited me to preach for a week. We started on a Tuesday night in a driving rain and went from a small crowd to a packed tent in three nights.

The meeting steamrolled. On the weekend crowds were lining the tent on all sides. Some miraculous healings had stirred the city. On the closing night of the first week, Steve insisted that the meeting continue. (It finally went on for nine weeks before I had to close it from sheer exhaustion.) I began to get mail from people throughout the nation requesting me to come to their bedside and pray for them. They offered to fly me out and even pay me sums of money. Naturally, I could not accept. And invitations from pastors and churches to conduct similar meetings began to flow in.

I knew that I was on God's time line. Then something happened that was to be an omen of events to come. For unknown reasons, a man in the area wanted to see the meeting closed. He'd been before the city council trying to get our license revoked. He had made wild accusations with uncontrollable anger. Steve Pringle had gone to visit with him but nothing helped. The man was determined that the meeting would not continue, but we did not know how determined he was.

During the service one night he stood across the street with a .45 revolver and fired it at me. The bullet whipped past my ear missing me by less than eighteen inches. A small hole showed where it had pierced the tent.

My evangelistic ministry had almost ended before it began. The next day the news services picked up the story and it was carried throughout the nation. From that day until this, controversy has dogged my every step.

There have been times I've wanted to cry out against unfair and inaccurate reports. Other times I just wished for quiet and solace.

Yet despite how much every person wants to be accepted by the establishment and leaders of the nation, I have known deep within that this could never be for me. God called me to a ministry to the needy and not to those with plenty. He called me to the desperate and the dying, not the happy and the contented. He called me to minister to the elderly people, sick people, people in pain and poverty. He called me to minister to those who have reached the extremities of their existence, who are facing the awful chasm and who need to hear a word of hope and see a ray of light. A world of suffering humanity was to be my parish. It is in this arena that my life's work has been performed.

Despite knowing this, no amount of inner conviction or assurance of the rightness of my task ever prepared me for the viciousness of some of the attacks upon me. Though they have varied in strength and in intensity, perhaps the most vicious reaction was during my ministry overseas in Australia.

When the invitation first came in 1954, I had no inkling of the reaction we would later encounter. Australia seemed like a natural place for me to minister. The people speak English, so there would be no language barrier. I've always found translators difficult to work with. Too, there was a unity among the pastors that promised exciting results.

Our ministry had been on the radio in Australia for several years. The number of subscriptions to our magazine and the amount of mail we were getting from Australia were continuing to grow.

The plans for the meeting were over two years in the making. We shipped the big tent, the trucks, and equipment over on boats several weeks before the meetings were to start.

We left America with great anticipation, and when we

arrived at the airport in Sydney, Australia, we received a gracious welcome. Tears filled the eyes of many of the pastors as they welcomed us, for they were overjoyed that we had consented to come, bringing our tent and all of our equipment, and our crusade team. The city fathers were present. *Seemingly*, everything was being done to insure a meaningful crusade effort.

But before the first night's service could begin, hostile, inaccurate stories came out in the papers attacking the "Yankee faith-healer." Then when we did start the first service, the pastors were shocked at the way the Australian reporters conducted themselves. Photographers crouched down in front of the pulpit for an unfavorable expression. They refused to move when requested, despite the fact that in the prayer line people from all denominations came seeking help. Virtually every church in the country was represented. Miracles began to happen.

Apparently because of this, the press opposition began to subside. The people filled the tent and by the week's end, over twenty-five hundred had come forward to accept Christ as their Savior.

Most of us on the team felt we had overcome the opposition in Australia and that when we went to Melbourne we could look forward to a most significant ministry. It was to be everything but that. In fact, I had no idea I would have to flee for my life.

We went to Melbourne shortly after the Sydney crusade closed. On opening night over ten thousand people filled the big tent. Four hundred came forward to give their lives to Christ. Many miracles occurred in the healing line—this despite there being a number of persons yelling and ridiculing during the service.

In Sydney, when this had happened, the police had stepped in with strength and the hecklers soon began to lose courage. But in Melbourne the police stood by watching and making no attempt whatever to quell the disturbances. The ministers protested. It did no good.

Egged on by their success and the continuing vicious attacks from the press, the second night was bedlam. The press had attacked us virulently and the protestors took this as their license to do just about anything they pleased.

Order was almost impossible to keep. What had originally been fifty or more hecklers gradually grew to hundreds. They stationed themselves throughout the tent and at the entrances. They hooted, jeered, yelled, and disturbed us with increasing ferocity.

When I gave the altar call and invited the unsaved to come forward, young hoodlums ran around through the tent trying to persuade the people not to go forward. Two hundred and fifty came forward anyhow. Then when I started to pray, every time I said a word they started a chorus of yells.

There was little doubt in my mind when the service ended that we were headed for a crisis. But despite the opposition I had preached both nights with an unusually strong anointing and freedom.

The press intensified their attacks. They printed supposed interviews with my associates and me that had never taken place. Now and then a courteous reporter would come and we would talk, and he would assure me that a fair story would be written. We would search the papers in vain for his articles. The most that ever appeared which was favorable was a little two-inch story that was lost in the middle of a paper.

On the front page of one of the largest papers a cartoon appeared showing me with a huge mouth and dressed like a hillbilly. The caption underneath read: "Thar's gold in them thar ills." The truth was that by prearrangement the expenses for the crusade team were all being borne by our American office. The offerings were to go directly to the sponsoring pastors' association for their ministry and follow-up after we left. I was not to receive one thin dime from any of the offerings received.

The next day the local ministers went to the city officials to complain about the lack of police protection. The magistrate told them there was no law to cover religious meetings unless there was violence. When the ministers told them what was going on in the tent each night and proved to them it was violence, the man in charge simply shrugged his shoulders and declined to reply.

I went to the American consul's office. The consul sympathized and tried to be helpful, but he told us that there was such bitter anti-Americanism in the Melbourne press there was nothing he could do to help. He recommended that for our own safety we leave and close the crusade. I was unwilling to have this happen.

In Sydney we had stayed at one of the leading hotels, and the press had viciously attacked this luxury. Because of their attack, I elected in Melbourne to stay in a private home. That was a bigger mistake.

Night and day, hecklers and reporters camped around

the house, yelling epithets and curses. Soon they were threatening my life, and promising they would "get" me.

By Wednesday night's service the violence was well organized. Leading Communist party troublemakers were on hand. Any call for order brought immediate threats and intimidations.

Thursday night the opposition was a screaming mob. In an attempt to answer the opposition the press had raised, as a part of that night's service, one of Melbourne's elected councilmen had been selected to ask questions posed by the press.

He and I stood before the vast audience and he began to fire away. One by one I answered each question as best I could. The audience of thousands began to cheer and applaud me. When the hecklers saw the tide turning against them they became incensed. They turned on their own councilman in rage. Stink bombs were set off. Someone attempted to set fire to the tent.

When I preached and gave the invitation for the unsaved to come forward, young hoodlums physically forced people to sit down and blocked their way to the front. Still forty brave souls made their way forward. I've never felt more admiration for anyone taking a step toward God than for those forty.

There was now little I could do. Hooligans blocked access to the prayer line and ridiculed anyone who got through. The mob was out to get me and they felt their opportunity was at hand. When the service was finally dismissed, local ministers feared for my life and advised me to go by a different route and in a different car to my lodging.

As we started to leave, I looked back and saw the car I normally rode in being rocked back and forth as the mob sought to turn it over.

Suddenly I said, "Where is my wife?"

When they told me she was in the car they were attacking, I was furious that I had consented to leave separately. I had thought surely someone would take care of her.

I said, "Stop this car! I'm getting out. Mob or no mob I will not leave my wife alone."

The ministers grabbed my arm and one of them said, "Brother Roberts, they will not hurt your wife. They are not interested in her. It is Oral Roberts they want. You must stay in this car if you value your life!" About that time one of the mob discovered that I was not in the car they were rocking. They immediately stopped their attack and began shouting in rage and frustration that I had eluded them.

"Wait till tomorrow night," they yelled.

Early the next morning Bob DeWeese, my associate evangelist, saw the headlines in the paper. It read: ROBERTS TENT TO BE BURNED.

The insurance company was contacted. They advised Bob to get the tent out of the city immediately. They did not want to pay for a forty-thousand-dollar loss.

Because of getting to bed after midnight, I did not awaken until 10 A.M. By that time Bob DeWeese had the tent taken down and loaded on our trucks to take to the ship. He also had made our reservations on the plane to Tulsa. He telephoned me and said, "Oral, get packed, we're leaving for home."

I said, "We are?"

He said, "Yes. I've met with the pastors and closed the crusade; the tent has been dismantled and is being put on the ship right now."

Then he told me what had been planned by the hoodlums. As we winged our way over the Pacific returning to the friendly shores of America I pondered over my visit to Australia. I loved those people. I felt that my ministry had been interrupted and many good people had been prevented from being helped. But it was beyond my control and I knew that it was in better hands than mine.

On the Friday night following the closing of the crusade, Melbourne's most respected news commentator and analyst, Norman Banks, devoted his broadcast to the meeting. He had been present on the final night. His words were a searing indictment of the violence that had occurred.

The following Monday night he added these comments:

> On Friday night last I said all that I wish to say about Oral Roberts' shameful treatment in Melbourne, but I thought you might be interested to learn, or to have recalled for you, the dramatic Atlantic meeting of Churchill and Roosevelt in August 1941.
>
> At that historic rendezvous, when these two great democrats got together to plan for a better future for all mankind, a fundamental base for their Atlantic Charter was the American President's speech of January of the same year, in which he said:
> "In future days we will look forward to the four

essential freedoms—freedom of speech and expression everywhere; the freedom of every person, and the right to worship God in their own way everywhere; freedom from want; and freedom from fear."

We Melbournians should never be led away from this high ideal. Freedom of religion for everyone is just as important as freedom from want and fear, as freedom of speech.

Many months after that experience in Australia I did some deep soul searching. In America my ministry was growing at a phenomenal rate and yet in one week an overseas crusade had been stopped cold by vicious mobs.

Today in our land someone has stated that violence "is as American as apple pie." By many barometers we do lead the world in murders, assaults, robbery, and acts of violence. Too, there is a social upheaval and discontent among the poor and the disfranchised that is taking violent form. The youth of our land are questioning our intents and national commitment.

Though I have a visceral reaction to violence and mob action, I know there can be legitimate protests against inequities. But ever since I almost lost my life through mob violence, I've been forced to work through my own attitudes toward public protest and reached the basic conclusion that no lasting and legitimate change in any system in any country has ever been brought about by people who didn't love their country despite its errors.

Much of the organized violence in America today—the bombings and murders—comes from people who have grown to hate this land. They are out to destroy everything, good or bad.

And I feel we cannot afford to ignore the intentions of those who would destroy us. Yet in responding to them we must be true to ourselves, to our laws, to our constitution, and to our principles.

In our relationships with overseas countries it is a blot on our national character that at this very moment we are supporting dictators and despots simply because of their alignment with us in defense treaties. Young people do not listen to what we say, but react to what they see. I feel certain that if our foreign affairs would begin to reflect our nation's commitment, much of the resistance and protest of our youth would subside.

Recently, Senator Mark Hatfield of Oregon spent a day on our campus. For several years the Senator has been a friend of this ministry and always received us graciously in our visits to Oregon while he was governor.

While speaking to our faculty cabinet at Oral Roberts University, he expressed some things that I believe in very strongly. He said: "Our foreign aid has failed primarily because we have wanted credit. We have not given because it was right. We've done it because we thought it was politically advantageous. If we would give our charity not for purpose of acclaim, if we gave it anonymously through multi-national groups without putting stamped USA, we would get probably far greater results."

That's what I call seed-faith giving . . . giving unto God for Him to use and expect Him to multiply.

Not too long ago I was asked to speak at a naturalization ceremony in Tulsa for new American citizens. The presiding judge, one of the Southwest's most distinguished jurists, was the Honorable Allen E. Barrow. Here is an excerpt of the address (which I gave extemporaneously and without notes; later a tape of it was sent to me):

Your Honor, ladies and gentlemen, and especially our new citizens.

As I watched you walk forward and receive your new Certificates of Citizenship I could feel the lumps coming in your throats because I could feel the one in mine. I would like to share with you today, not a prepared speech or one which I should read, but one coming out of my own heart, an experience as an American, as an Oklahoman.

Ever since the Tower of Babel, when the languages of man were confused and mankind was scattered throughout the earth, man has looked for a home. In looking for a home, he has encountered many difficulties, most of which were designed to help him develop himself as a human being, as a good citizen, and as a person who is concerned not only with himself, but everybody around him.

It is not known for certain but as far as we can determine, the American Indian was the first immigrant to the United States, having crossed, as we believe, from Asia into Alaska, where he began to travel in his nomadic wanderings throughout what later became Canada, United States, Mexico and various parts of Latin America. He was here for centuries, finding or ever seeking to find his place.

In the early 1600s a few Europeans came to this broad land and encountered the Indian people. Some of them were friendly; some of them were not, and not long afterwards, scattered wars began to break out across the continent; and then there began a merging, almost intangible at first, but a merging that took definite shape between the red man and the white man.

Ultimately, immigrants came from Asia, the black man from Africa, and later South America, and in this country we have had the first great melting pot of mankind.

As time went on, colonies were formed until thirteen of them organized into a Federation. They joined together in writing a Constitution and bringing forth a new kind of government where man would be looked upon, not for his country or for the fact that he was born to a certain family, but looked upon for himself, as a human being, with certain rights conferred upon him by Almighty God, and by these thirteen colonies.

In 1776, these colonies declared their independence.

In 1789, they ratified the new Constitution, and thereafter, with the Bill of Rights, they rectified one of their mistakes.

They gave to this country Freedom of Speech; and I know how valuable Freedom of Speech is, because I have been in places where I was denied Freedom of Speech.

They gave the Freedom of Press, and I have been the recipient of the blessings of the press and the recipient of the other end of the press. I can value the Freedom of the Press.

The Freedom of Religion, without which I could not have developed as a human being with rights and privileges.

The Freedom of Assembly. When I think of the crusades we have conducted throughout this land, with crowds ranging up into the tens of thousands I can testify to the blessing of Freedom of Assembly.

And then the Due Process of Law, where every man had his right to be judged according to the law, not the bias or the prejudice or the bitterness or the hate of anyone, whether his group be large or small, where he could come into a court and could state his case. I have been on that spot too, and I appreciate the Due Process of Law in this land, for I have been in certain lands where my rights were taken away, and I was judged without a trial and almost lost my life.

So, growing up in this land, the Bill of Rights has meant everything to me, and as you encounter this from day to day and month to month and year to year, you will come to a reality of it in a way that you have not been able to realize only by a study of its principles.

In the 1860s, this country was divided by a vast and terrible Civil War. It was a war fought for the freedom of the Negroes who had been enslaved in this country for scores of years. It was also a battle of States' Rights, a battle that is still being fought this day that you have become a citizen of the United States.

A great President told us, "Four score and seven years ago our fathers brought forth on this continent a new nation, conceived in liberty and dedicated to the proposition that all men are created equal."

The blood of tens of thousands of people was shed that that might become a reality. It has not yet become a full reality, and it is with hope that we look at you that you may help us with this and other problems.

This country has been involved in foreign wars. In 1917 and '18, in 1941 through '45, and in Korea in the fifties, and now in a war in Vietnam, in which a half million of our sons are involved, a war that few of us understand. Even having been there and traveled up and down that land and talked and prayed with scores and hundreds of men from generals down to privates, my own understanding is very small of what is going on in Vietnam. Man is in trouble.

Along with the greatness of this land, there are weaknesses, one of which is the lack of ability to find ways to live with our fellowman. But we are not alone in that problem. All the nations of the world are battling with it. But out of all this has come a nation where the ethnic groups have attempted to merge, and I think we have done a pretty good job. In less than two hundred years of formal government, we have law, we have religion, we have a press, we have the ability to say what is in our hearts, we have the ability to grow and develop and become decent and respectable human beings.

Let me change the format just a moment and to share a little with you concerning Oklahoma.

Oklahoma means "Red Man." At one time, more than seventy different Indian tribes lived in America. Remnants of all those tribes remain. Some of them have been moved farther west, particularly to Mexico and Arizona.

But, in the early part of the last century, the Five Civilized Tribes were moved to Oklahoma; the Cherokees, the Chickasaws, the Choctaws, the Seminoles, and Creeks; coming from the east and the south of our country, pushed out by the white man.

You may have read about the Trail of Tears. Many of these Indian people died on the way from Georgia, Alabama, Tennessee, and other places back east and south.

But here in Oklahoma, they formed governments, almost like a foreign power within this nation. There was a Cherokee government, the Creek government, and we are now seated and standing on old Indian territory. Not far from here is where the Cherokee and the Creek joined together, I imagine not more than a mile or two miles from this Court House.

By 1835 they were living at peace, they enforced their laws, and there was virtually no crime among these Five Civilized Tribes.

And then the ·white man came. Soon there was war between the white man and the red man. The white man multiplied back east and wanted to push the frontier back toward the West, and he came to Oklahoma, which was known as "Indian Territory." Parts of it became known as the bad lands.

We have a section in the southeastern part of the state called the Cookson Hills, where many of these people who came in hid out and went out on their forages of destruction.

Eventually the white man made a law that he could take over this land of Oklahoma, and there were great land runs in the 1890s. Millions of acres were opened up so that people coming from all of our states, and even from overseas, came to a starting point, and at high noon when a gun was fired, these people on horseback or wagons or carriages, or however, made a race toward 160 acres, a quarter of a section of land, where the first one who drove his stake would receive a deed to that land.

There is a special quality about Oklahoma, because it too is a mixing land. It is where the various ethnic groups of the whole nation have converged, along with the red man, and have tried to bring forth a new kind of life. They were forced upon the land. The conditions were primitive.

My people came into Oklahoma in 1892. I was born eleven years after Oklahoma became a state in 1907.

Our fathers and our grandfathers came into this state when it was raw and primitive; when the grass was almost up to your waist; when covies of quail were so numerous that two to three hundred would swarm at one time. It was a land of animals; of waving grass. It was a land where the Indian roamed free.

But out of it came a mixing of the ethnic groups and terrific individuality. That was partly because our people had to depend upon the land. First they dug holes in the ground until they could build a soddy or a little frame house. They had no schools and no churches, and eventually when schools were formed you went by horseback or walked. Even I, as a small child, walked three and four miles to a little one-room schoolhouse.

The winters were cold and the summers were hot. The food was scarce and the neighbors were few and far between.

My father and grandfather used to regale me with stories of the Indians who would surround our house. Our houses always had an opening so that a gun could be put out and shot. Those stories are real.

But, having been forced upon the land to use our hands, we found ourselves on the frontier, which is where you are today. We have Oklahoma established, we have the nation established.

Today we are on a new kind of frontier in America. There are no more land runs. Most of the ethnic groups are here. We worked out many of our problems but now we face a Frontier of the Mind and the Spirit, which is the most difficult area of all.

It is hard to develop a new land. You know what it means to leave your old country and cross the ocean coming to a new land. It is hard. But now we are on a new kind of frontier that challenges us and will challenge you.

The Frontier of Economics. We have a problem of feeding, not only ourselves, but our world. Every farmer in America produces the average food supply for thirty other people, whereas in many lands the farmer is hard pressed to produce food for himself and two other people. We have a problem, an economic problem, of feeding the world. Only new creative processes will help us solve the food problem of the world.

We have labor problems; capital problems. All of it can be summed up in an economic problem that challenges every person in America to find ways and means of solving it.

Another problem is the educational problem. You know, in most other lands education is only for the privileged few, but our forefathers believed that every child should receive an education. But now it is the dream of this country that every boy and girl should receive a college education.

I came up in this state. I was born the son of poor parents, of an itinerant preacher, but I believe that it was in this state that something was bred in me where by faith in God, by initiative and hard work, I could accomplish whatever God had put in my heart. Oral Roberts University is one example.

Another frontier is in religion. A new spirit of ecumenicity, or a new spirit of family is coming into our country where we are not divided as we once were by sectarianism. Where each man can worship God and respect the other man as he worships God, eliminating bitterness and prejudice. We respect one another, but still keep our faith in God.

I am very happy about this development. That does not take away from your faith or from your relationship with your church, but it does mean that we respect the other man.

Another frontier is in the realm of healing. I mention that because of man's illnesses. The illnesses of his body, the illnesses of his mind, and most of all, those in spirit. Finding new ways in medical healing, in spiritual healing, in the healing that comes to people by just simply love and understanding. We are on a Frontier of Healing.

We are on a Frontier of Finding New Ways of Peace, because we have not found the way to live in peace, and if there is a prayer that any of us should pray, I think the prayer should be:

> "Oh, God, give me peace in my heart and help me share that peace with at least one more person in my world."

As one person born in America and Oklahoma, I want to tell you how proud I am to watch you walk up here today and receive your new Certificate of Citizenship. You may think that means more to you than it does to us. It could not possibly do so. For we love America, we are a part of America, and we are honored that you chose us and you are a part of us.

Our late President Kennedy reminded the nation: "Ask not what your country can do for you, but what you can do for your country." You are going to gain by giving; by giving of yourself, by becoming involved with our problems; and recognizing that America is not everything. It has its limitations. Add yourself to the battle and help us to bring forth the right kind of country.

Finally, we have given you our name. Will you give us yours?

We have given you our heart. Will you give us yours?

We have given you our land. Will you give us yours?

We give you our prayers. Will you give us yours?

Thank you.

CHAPTER 8

Black vs. White

In my first tent crusade in Durham, North Carolina, in 1948 I was confronted with racial controversy. In fact, the white-black conflict was so great that only a few blacks were permitted to attend and they had to sit in a small segregated section. It seemed the only alternative I had was either to minister to whites only or close down and go home.

But I knew that God had not called me to do either. I finally decided to have special services for blacks only in addition to the all-white services. At these services, white people were not allowed. It was a compromise at best, but it made a witness to both races.

When we set the first service for the blacks I had no idea how many of them would want to attend the meeting. I arrived that night about eight o'clock and the service was in progress. It seemed as though ten thousand people were singing. I jumped out of the car and ran as fast as I could to the tent. I saw that it was packed with black people. Many were standing along the outside edges.

I had never seen so many black people gathered in one place in my life. When the man in charge found I was there, he signaled the audience. They had planned to sing "Shine on Me" in my honor. When I got up on the platform, they started, and their voices were like the voices of angels. From their throats and hearts rolled forth the beautiful words of "Shine on me, shine on me. Let the light from the lighthouse shine on me."

I remember that I looked straight up to the top of the tent. I would not have been surprised if a shaft of light from Heaven had shone all the way from Glory to that earthly place. I felt chills going up and down my spine. It seemed all of Heaven broke loose and the glory of the Lord filled that place.

I was told that sixty-three black ministers were present and had brought their congregations.

I started preaching. As I did, it seemed that they reached out with their hands and pulled me to their hearts. Every word I said was received by them. The place roared with their amens and hallelujahs. I began to gather speed as they said amen to me. When I had preached about an hour, I felt I was losing my voice, for as they got louder, I got louder. Presently I stopped and said, "People, if you don't quit saying amen to me I will preach myself to death." They laughed but just kept on saying amen. The "preach" rolled out of me that night like rivers of water.

When I gave the invitation, over three hundred came

down the aisles to be saved. Following the altar call, we announced that I would pray for as many sick as were there. It seemed as if everybody in the tent was sick. More than a thousand people rose and came forward to be healed. I didn't know what in the world I would do with such a large group of sick people. I started in praying for them one by one. I got so tired I had to grit my teeth, but I held on. I was determined to pray for every one of them.

As they came before me in the prayer line I told them I would lay my right hand upon them and say a brief prayer for their healing and I would expect the Lord to heal them. I asked them to believe through that point of contact.

But I was not accustomed to such physical demonstrations, and when they came before me and I touched them on the head with my hand and prayed a brief prayer some jumped as though they had been shot. Others jumped straight up and down, some ran out of my arms down through the crowd waving their hands and shouting, some fell down on the floor. I couldn't tell by these demonstrations if they were healed or not. Presently, however, a young woman brought her blind son. Never shall I forget her. What she said almost tore the heart out of me. She was saying, "Oh, Lord, I just want him to see. Oh, Lord, I just want him to see." Turning her eyes upon me, she said, "Man of God, I'm not asking much, I just want him to see."

I thought my heart would burst from my body. I looked into that child's sightless eyes and the tears streamed down my face like water. His young mother began to

sway before me, chanting her pleading prayer, "Oh, Lord,
I just want him to see."

When I touched his eyes with my hand and prayed,
it seemed as if I touched a live wire. The child screamed,
"I can see! I can see!" The little mother shook with joy
and that entire crowd jumped to their feet. They began
to jerk their bodies and wave their hands. Some were crying, some were shouting, some were singing. I had them
all stop and sing "Shine on Me." There was drama, pathos,
and joy all through the audience. It was an unforgettable
experience.

In that first tent crusade in 1948 we established a pattern that was important. I refused to accept the limitation
of a whites-only ministry and at every opportunity I
sought to give witness to this commitment.

But the times were changing and methods of compromise and amelioration became more and more difficult to
find. Gradually, what had become fragmented pockets of
resistance began to be organized. Racial conflict began
to fill the nation's newspapers. Sit-ins, demonstrations,
protests, and violence began to sweep the South.

In the heat of this controversy, I went to another large
southern city to conduct a crusade. Our ministry had
many friends there and from all preliminary reports it
looked as if we would have one of our most successful
crusades.

The crusade team had been working with the local
pastors for months in advance. Much publicity and planning had gone into the effort. Scores of churches were
holding prayer services as preparation for a large evangel-

2. Oral and his brother Vaden.

3. The Pentecostal Holiness Church, Enid, Oklahoma, the last church Oral Roberts served as a pastor.

4. Oral and Evelyn Roberts with their oldest daughter, Rebecca, and her two daughters.

5. Oral Roberts with his parents at Fresno, California, crusade.

6. Until 1968 the big tent was home for nearly all Oral Roberts crusades.

7. During a service in Amarillo, Texas, in 1950, a tornado-like storm toppled the big tent, but miraculously none of the 7,000 worshipers was seriously hurt.

istic thrust. When I arrived, I met with the pastors and shared with them some of the things I hoped to see achieved. Then that afternoon we had the first service with my associate evangelist, Bob DeWeese, conducting the service.

Bob's a big man, a former athlete, and a powerful and happy preacher. There is a joy in his sermons that radiates a Christ-like life. But Bob later related to me that as he began this service he saw pockets of movement and heard low rumbles and murmurings. The disturbance continued throughout the service—so much so that he thought the service was almost ruined.

As soon as the meeting was dismissed, he immediately began to inquire from the ushers and the crusade team what was wrong. But before he could get all the information, people began to encircle him and to complain.

Finally Bob got them all quiet and asked what in the world had happened.

"The niggers are trying to sit with the whites!"

Bob was born and raised on the West Coast and because of the small number of blacks in Washington and Oregon he had never had to deal, as a pastor, with this issue before. But as he listened suddenly a black woman moved in close and said, "Brother DeWeese, we are God's children just as much as any white folks. We've got a right to sit in the same place as the white man."

In just a few minutes the conflict that was gripping our nation and is still a smoldering giant was about to disrupt our crusade.

Things began to get hot. Centuries of prejudice and frustration were exploding in miniature in Bob's face.

Finally, one old black woman brought everything to a halt. With a note of triumph in her voice she said, "Wait till Brother Roberts gets here. He won't treat us this way."

With that the crowd dispersed and immediately Bob started trying to get in touch with me. That wasn't easy to do, for in order to have time to prepare for the service that night I had told the hotel operator not to put any calls through. Bob tried in vain to persuade her differently.

Finally he drove over to the hotel and came up to my room. Quite frankly, when I heard his knock on the door it irritated me. I had decided very early in my ministry if I were going to be effective when preaching to thousands at night I could not spend time visiting and talking to person after person during the day. My usual routine was to spend from two-thirty to seven-thirty each day by myself in prayer and preparation.

I opened the door and immediately Bob said, "Oral, we've got a problem."

I replied, "Bob, I've got a problem, too. I have to preach tonight and pray for people, many of whom are dying, to be healed. You're interrupting my preparation." Bob was ready for that because he had been one of the first to insist that I should have time alone before the services. He and others on the team shouldered completely the organization of the meetings and the mechanics of the crusades.

Undaunted, he said, "Oral, I know, but we're having a little racial problem that could very well get out of hand."

When he said that I knew it was not something to be

taken lightly. I was completely floored and irritated—irritated at Bob for interrupting me and irritated that our crusade was now being threatened.

I started to invite Bob in to discuss the problem. Then I decided against it. I asked him instead to plan a meeting that night with the ministers and the crusade team and after the service we would get together and see what could be done.

He left and I started trying to finish my sermon and put my mind again on God and the needs of the people. It wasn't too easy, but finally I felt the assurance I needed and by the time the service was to begin I was ready to go.

As our car approached the tent, I suddenly saw what was happening. There were placards protesting discrimination and small crowds milling around the edge of the tent. When I saw them, I couldn't believe it.

Though raised in the South and Southwest, I had never felt that I personally was racially prejudiced. I had always had a deep concern for people in need—poor people, sick people, black people, Indians, and any man on the short end of the stick. To me the whole Gospel was for people in need. One of the scriptures that had moved me the most as I entered this ministry was Jesus' proclamation in Luke 4:18:

> The Spirit of the Lord is upon me, because he hath anointed me to preach the gospel to the poor; he hath sent me to heal the brokenhearted, to preach deliverance to the captives, and recovering of sight to the blind, to set at liberty them that are bruised.

For me that meant all people in need—black, white, red, yellow, brown—and all shades between.

Now, however, the service had already started and there was little time to investigate the cause of the placards. So I went to the platform and heard several of the local dignitaries being introduced on this first night of the service. We had a hymn and then Bob DeWeese introduced me.

I had decided while riding from the hotel that it would not be wise to try and solve this problem from the pulpit— one-way dialogues seldom help any situation. So I went right into my sermon. God anointed me and I preached with as much freedom and assurance as ever. Yet I could sense that the audience was not reacting in quite the same way as they normally did.

I finished the sermon and gave an invitation for those who needed Christ to come forward to the front. Suddenly, at the altar of God, an ugly racial drama began to unfold. The problem was this: never before in this city had integrated services occurred. There was an ordinance against it. In every service there was always a place for the white people to sit and then in the back a place for the blacks. This same arrangement held true even at the altar. Whites went forward and prayed at one part of the altar and the blacks went over to another part.

Now before me some of the blacks had come down with the whites and instead of moving over to their section, they were standing with the whites at the altar.

I must be honest and admit that this type of segregation had occurred in many of our crusades in the South before, but because there was no protest, we had never thought much about it. I guess I had consoled myself with thinking, "That's just the way things are."

But through this incident God was showing me that because things are the way they are, does not mean they are the way they should be.

Again, though, I knew I couldn't solve this problem at the mike. I tried to ignore the conflict I saw before me. I asked everyone to join with me in a sinner's prayer. Then I offered a prayer myself and sat down. Bob took over and directed each one to the prayer counselors.

I went to the invalid room to pray for the extremely ill and then came back and began prayer for those who had formed the healing line.

I prayed for a long line of people that night and many seemed to be helped. Yet everytime a black person came before me it seemed that there was a change in the service—a deep brooding omen of worse things to come.

Immediately following the service, I went to meet with Bob and the local preachers. These men were fine men, many of them were pastoring outstanding churches with a sincere love for God and His people. Yet they, too, were subject to the same prejudices we all had been raised in. After much discussion, the issue resolved to this: there was a city ordinance that prohibited integrated seating in the services. Blacks must sit in a different section from the whites. Bob had been in touch with the local authorities and they had informed him that if trouble broke out because of our allowing integrated seating, the law officials would be forced to close the services and fine us for breaking the law. That meant even altar services had to be segregated.

I left the meeting with no final decision made on what to do. The next afternoon Bob instructed the ushers to seat the blacks in a separate section from the whites. The whites liked it, the blacks didn't. In fact, some of the blacks left in protest. That night the same instructions were given to the ushers regarding the seating. The service then went as usual. I preached my sermon and then started to make the altar call. But instead of saying anything I just stood there with my head down and my hands behind me. It got so quiet you could hear the slightest little sound.

Then I looked up and began to talk softly.

"In a few minutes I'm going to invite those who want to be saved to come forward. But before I do I want to say this:

"We've been having something happen here that's never happened in one of my crusades before. A lot of hate is being stirred up. Some of you white people are upset that black people are trying to sit in the white section. Some of you black people are angry because you feel you are being mistreated.

"And last night when I gave the altar call, instead of people rejoicing to see souls saved, I saw that many of you were angry because blacks and whites were mixing here at the altar.

"I've made my decision on what we're going to do."

It really got quiet then. Every eye in the tent was on me. It seemed even as if the babies had stopped crying and the small children no longer were moving about. And then I told them my decision.

"The law says that whites must be seated in one section

and the blacks in another. In this meeting we are going to follow the law."

And then I paused. You could see the reaction of the crowd. Many white folks were now smiling and whispering to each other. I looked over to the black people and they looked defeated. Some were shaking their heads in disbelief, some were crying and some were staring straight at me with anger on their faces.

I asked for their attention.

"I want every one of you to know that I believe God loves everyone the same, whatever his color. And He wants to save you whatever your color. I want you to listen closely. Even though there is a forced segregated seating, when I invite you to come forward to be saved there will be no separation of black and white here at God's altar."

Suddenly the tide turned. Some whites looked in unbelief and the blacks were no longer scowling.

"I defy any person in this service or any official of this city to try and force the altar of God to be segregated. Everyone who steps forward comes to this altar as a sinner, not as a black or a white person. When he leaves this altar, if he has repented of his sins and God has forgiven him those sins, he returns to his seat as a sinner saved by grace regardless if his skin is black or white. Any person who chooses to come forward tonight and wants to stand here at this altar—either end or middle—can do so."

Then I gave the invitation and the people started coming forward. It seemed to me that nearly every black under the tent was unsaved now and wanted to be a Christian. I'm sure a lot of them just wanted to experience

an integrated altar service, but there were some of them
who wept their way through to Christ.

I'll be the first, though, to admit that what I did was a
compromise and it wasn't a perfect solution. The white
attendance did drop some, the number of white prayer
counselors declined, but it seemed that we had made a
witness that was to become increasingly important. Remember this was in the early fifties.

Because of this experience, in our future crusades we
no longer even considered permitting segregated seating.
And if those who invited our crusades to their cities insisted on segregated seating, we simply declined their
invitation. It was a breakthrough not only of conscience,
but common sense. It was the right thing to do and we
did it.

This same policy has continued to hold for all of our
ministry, especially at Oral Roberts University. It has
been integrated from the first day of classes and it has
been from this experience at ORU with black and white
students that I have developed my deepest insight to the
racial problem that we are facing in this land.

Recently we had a black heritage week at ORU during
which time I was asked to make an address. Specifically,
I was requested to share my views on interracial dating
and intermarriage. Here is what I told them as taken from
the taping of the talk:

> When you begin to date a person that's not of your
> race or you marry such a person, you've got to ask
> yourself at least three questions.

First, have I the courage to inform my mother and father? You might say, "Well, what business is it of theirs? I'm now an adult and can make my own choices. My parents were responsible for their dating and marriage and I will be for mine. Whether or not I go with a person of another race is my decision to make!"

The Bible says, "Honor thy father and thy mother that thy days may be long upon the earth." Your parents may say, "Yes." Or they may say, "No." The point is that they love you enough that they should know. They shouldn't have to find out secondhand.

The other night my mother had to be taken to the emergency ward of the hospital. She's eighty-five and we thought she was passing that night. Thank God she didn't go. I got up in the middle of the night and went to the hospital and spent some time with her and prayed for her. Then as morning was approaching I got into my car and started back home. That's really when you begin to think about your parents. Maybe you should have thought about them more before, but you really think when your mother or father may be losing their life. I tell you, you've got to honor your parents. Whether you agree with them or disagree with them has nothing to do with it. It's just basic humanity.

The second question you have to ask yourself is this: would I date that person if he were not a different color? Am I dating him because he is who he is or just because his color is different from mine? Is my going with him a gimmick, a fetish, or a fad? If it is, you're not real. That's not Christianity. That's not humanity. It's not real. And don't think the other person doesn't know it. He knows whether he is an object or whether you are concerned or you respect him.

Would I go with him if he were my color or am I just going with him because he's white or red or black? Am I going because he's the human being I respect and I want to be with?

The third question is this: am I willing and am I ready to face the social implications of this act? Because they won't vanish, let me tell you. I'm here to inform you that the human race is not going to change because you suddenly start dating someone of a different color. The human race is rejecting God. I'm here to tell you that there is a minority of people in the human race that will accept Jesus and take His cross, but the great majority won't do it. You have to be willing to face the attitudes of people, attitudes which have been built up and nourished for centuries, attitudes that are wrong. You've got to face it. You will suffer over it and if you suffer over it you have to suffer for joy or it's not the cross. If you suffer out of bitterness it's not the cross. This is really basic Christianity.

This nation is not a Christian nation and you can knock your brains out getting mad about it, but people are going to be like that. Some of them will be church folks. But faith is where you find it, whether it's in a church building or outside one.

The best way I know to show honor and respect to my black brother this week is to do it every week. We are brothers. I feel that way about my sons and daughters and their relationship with the yellow man, the red man, the black man, or the brown man, or the white man.

I feel encouraged at ORU. We've got a long way to go. Some on our campus make interdating a fad on both sides and they suffer. The price is too big to pay but if it's really inside you, if you really do it as part of your love for Christ and your brother, it will work and you can look anybody in the eye without bitterness and say, "This is what God wants me to do."

This talk really expresses the way I feel.

As we were building the physical plant at Oral Roberts University in the early sixties we applied for a federal construction loan. Soon afterwards we received a call from the Office of Education in Washington, D.C. They wanted to know what our policy on racial integration would be.

I assured them that from the very first day of school ORU would be integrated and we have kept that promise. And anyone who visits our campus soon discovers how true it is.

For the blacks on our campus have not been relegated only to athletics, but they have participated in every segment of ORU's life. One of our first student body presidents was a young black man, Bob Goodwin. He was the unanimous choice of the entire student body.

In every traveling group we've had, both in America and overseas, there has always been a good representation of blacks as well as other ethnic groups.

When we went back on television I told my producer that I wanted our first special guest to be a black star. And I asked if at all possible that we get Mahalia Jackson.

Mahalia consented, came on the show and did a marvelous job. I had known Mahalia for years and had at times prayed for her over the phone when she was sick.

When she came to Tulsa for a concert, we had visited together. I had always been impressed with her witness and determination to use her voice for God.

But a lot of people did not think this way. We received many letters of criticism from church people for having her on the show. And a lot of them objected to the way I prayed for her. I had put my hands on her shoulders and prayed for her and she had done the same to me. We then joined hands in prayer for the people of all races and nations of the world.

Despite those objections, it was one of the most meaningful things we had done with blacks in some time. I received letters from blacks all over America who were blessed by the show. That show set the tone for every one we've had since. And it opened the door for us to use more black stars such as Lou Rawls, Stu Gilliam, Andrei Crouch, and others.

In Tulsa we have a savings and loan association owned by black people that has been having real difficulty. Because it did not have enough deposits on hand, it could not meet the minimum requirements for obtaining federal deposit insurance, and because it did not have insurance against loss, people were reluctant to deposit their money there. It was a vicious circle.

These people had been desperately searching for assistance. Finally, in New York, they were told, "Why don't you get Oral Roberts to help you?"

They phoned me and said, "Mr. Roberts, we went to New York and the people in New York said, 'Go back to Tulsa, and contact Oral Roberts. He will help you.'"

I asked, "How did they know me?"

They said, "We don't know. But they said you could help us." So I went over and met with them. They told me their problems. And as I listened they put before me a picture of three hundred years of injustice, discrimination, and misuse. There was a deep bitterness and resentment within them that was now surfacing over their inability to meet the white man's criteria for insurance. They had given to the white man for centuries; now he wouldn't help them even though he owed it to them.

After they finished, I asked them this question. I said, "Do you want me to be honest?"

"Oh yes, Dr. Roberts," they replied. "Tell it like it is."

"Okay," I said, "here it is like it is! You haven't given the white man anything."

It was as though I had slapped them across the face. I didn't have to wait for a reaction, for immediately they started to tell me of all they had given personally and what the black man as a race had been forced to give.

When they said that, I stopped them. I said, "That's the point—you were forced to give. You never gave on your own, it was taken from you. The right to work where you were qualified, to earn a fair salary, to live where you wanted, to send your children to the best schools—these rights were taken from you. You didn't give a one of them.

"Now, you feel that the white man owes you something. He's obligated to help you. And you resent that he's not doing it.

"Well, let me tell you, he not only isn't doing it now, he's not going to do it in the future.

"I know that's difficult to accept. I'm not saying he

doesn't owe you something, for certainly he does. The white man's oppression of the blacks is one of the most sordid chapters in America's history—and oppression is still going on.

"But you called me over here to help you and I want to help. I will call on as many friends as I have here in Tulsa to try and help. We will contact the Federal Deposit Insurance Corporation to see if some leniency can be permitted. But those are only Band-Aids on a more serious illness. I'll tell you how you can solve the problem."

They said, "How?"

I said, "First, who is your source? The Bible says, 'For my God shall supply all your need.' You are saying, my government shall do it. You are saying certain white people shall do it, but the Bible says my God shall do it. Who is your source? Whom do you trust?"

That caused a pause. Then I told them, "Jesus said, 'Give and it shall be given to you.'"

One of them said, "We've given for three hundred years. Everytime I see white people I think of something bad that one of them has done to me."

I said, "The Bible speaks of a root of bitterness and it will destroy whoever has it."

He said, "Well, what shall we do?"

I answered, "I can't tell you all the technical parts, but I can tell you what God said. God said that He would supply your needs but you must put Him first in your life. You must think of Him as your source and know that the answer will come from Him. Second, you must start giving. Whatever you do from this point on, whether it's forced or voluntary, in your heart give it as unto the Lord. Give it as a seed you plant to God. Give, and it shall be given to you. Give God your best, then ask Him for His best. The greater the sacrifice the greater the blessing."

Then I said, "Expect a miracle."

One of them laughed and said, "It will take the biggest miracle this nation has ever known."

I said, "God's in the miracle-working business. God can work a miracle.

"If we will start giving, if we will start loving, then people can live where they want to live, go to school where they want and work where they want. If we will sit down and give to each other, God will give us a miracle. Our nation will be born again."

Well, it was an interesting experience. They were fine men and we had an open exchange. It's probably one of the first times that any savings and loan officers had someone lay hands on them and pray for their business!

They have begun a turn around. One of the results has been that the editor of one of our leading papers in Tulsa did a series on them. Different white businesses started making deposits with them. And although their problems are not totally solved, they have started up the hill. And I feel they will make it.

For our nation as a whole, our problems with those with whom we differ will never be solved from the standpoint of legal obligation and duty alone. We must

have more equitable laws. We must. But the final answer
will come only when individual men and women of every
race start giving of themselves, and giving first as Jesus
taught and gave Himself as the example.

CHAPTER 9

My Friend, Billy Graham

I first heard Billy Graham in the late forties. I had just finished a crusade in Bakersfield, California, and was resting a few days before my next meeting.

While reading the Los Angeles *Times* I saw an ad telling of one of Billy Graham's crusades. Evelyn and I decided to drive down and attend one of his services.

When we arrived, we saw that he was holding his meeting in a big tent. Evelyn and I found a seat in the back and stayed for the entire service. We thoroughly enjoyed it.

Billy preached then, as he does now, hard-hitting, judgment-type sermons that produced real results. I was much impressed, but there was no occasion for us to meet personally.

The next time I heard of Billy was when the famous folk singer and songwriter Stuart Hamblen was converted in Billy's meeting. By this time the Hearst newspapers had begun to give extensive coverage to the Graham meetings. His crusades were packed. Still there was no occasion for us to meet.

In September of 1950 I took my tent to Amarillo, Texas, for a crusade. It was totally destroyed in a storm which caused a drastic revision in the schedule of crusades I had slated. Some friends in Tacoma, Washington, invited Evelyn and me to come visit them while another tent was being made. While we were there we learned that Billy was in Portland, Oregon, in a crusade. Quite frankly, the storm in Amarillo had emotionally drained me and I was not interested in going to Portland to attend any meeting.

My friend insisted and said that he had attended the crusade earlier and had personally met with Billy Graham. According to him, Billy was eager for me to come to the service. In fact, Billy had told them of attending my services in Florida in the early days of my ministry and that some of his relatives had been prayed for by me.

So Evelyn and I flew down to Portland and checked into one of the downtown hotels. We were just going out the door to hail a taxi to take us to the meeting when we ran into Billy.

He recognized me instantly and said, "Oral, how nice to see you. I want you to go with me to the services."

I replied, "Well, we will get a cab and come on out."

He responded, "No, come and go with me in our cab."

So we agreed. On the way to the services he said, "Now I want you to come to the back with me, sit on the platform, and then lead the audience in prayer."

I was struck then that Billy wasn't aware of the controversy over my ministry. Feeling this, I told him, "Billy, are you sure you want me to do that? A lot of people don't understand my work."

He answered, "Well, I was blessed when my song leader, Cliff Barrows, and I sat in the back of your crowd during your meetings in Florida and I have an aunt who was healed through your ministry. God has not given me that kind of ministry, but He has given it to you. I want you to lead in prayer."

I consented. When the man in charge announced that I was going to lead in prayer, you could read the surprise on the faces in the audience. As I prayed, every person in the audience looked and listened intently. It was an interesting little drama.

After the service many people came up to introduce themselves. Several pastors asked me about coming to Portland for a crusade. One woman came up and said she had cancer and wanted me to pray for her. I refused and told her that this was another man's meeting and I didn't feel I should pray for her there. I turned and walked away. She followed me and kept insisting. I said, "No, I can't do that."

In exasperation she pointed her finger at me and said, "Well, if you don't pray for me and I die before my time, God is going to hold you accountable."

Finally, I said I would do as she asked, but only if she would step out into the street. I told her I would still not pray for her on the grounds where the crusade was being held.

She agreed, and we stepped out into the street where I

put my hands on her and prayed a brief prayer. She began to rejoice and was as thrilled as could be and walked away happy.

Evelyn and I left and went to the restaurant in the hotel where we were staying. While we were eating, Billy and Ruth came in and joined us. Billy is a friendly, outgoing type of person, and we had a terrific time. There were areas of mutual concern and similar experiences and dreams that made for instant camaraderie.

Then years passed with no further contact between us. Our organizations grew, our crusades increased in size and effectiveness. And finally, in 1959 we met again. It was in Washington, D.C.

The Full Gospel Businessmen's Fellowship, a movement of thousands of laymen who had experienced the baptism of the Holy Spirit and speaking in tongues, had invited me to come to Washington to speak to them at their meeting in one of the large hotels. I had no idea that Billy Graham was staying in the same hotel.

It happened that we had a mutual friend attending the meeting at which I was speaking. On his own he decided it would be great if Oral Roberts and Billy Graham could get together. He contacted Billy and Billy told him to invite me up to his room. My friend thought this was wonderful news and that he had been involved in arranging an important event.

He found me and said, "Billy Graham's here in the hotel and he wants you to come up to his room."

Suddenly deep negative feelings washed over me. In the interim since our last meeting I'd been to Australia where I had experienced the greatest defeat of my ministry. My Melbourne crusade had to be closed midway because of the opposition from the press. Billy went for a crusade there later and scored a great success. His newspaper clippings were soaring in their praise. Mine had portrayed me as a fraud and a villain.

When I replied to my friend in the negative, he could not believe it. I said simply, "I'm sorry, I can't do that."

He was crushed. He couldn't believe that I wouldn't go. He tried to persuade and cajole. I ignored him. Finally he went to Billy's room and told him that I couldn't come.

Again Billy insisted. Again my friend found me. He told me that he had told Billy that I couldn't come but that Billy insisted on my coming anyway. He wanted very much to talk to me.

While in Australia, Billy had written me a letter saying, "I know that you had a rather difficult time here, yet for your encouragement I have met many people that were blessed through your God-anointed ministry." Apparently, he wanted to say this to me in person to encourage me. I still was adamant. My friend persisted. Finally I turned to him and looked him straight in the eye. I said, "I will not go to his room."

This time he heard me because he immediately stopped insisting. Evidently though, I had inflected "his room" because he now went to Billy and said that I wouldn't come to his room and would he come to mine. Again Billy said, "Yes, I very much want to see him." My friend again found me and said, "Billy wants to see you very much. Can he come to your room?"

Quietly, I replied, "If Billy wants to come to my room, I would be glad to have him."

Some of my close associates accompanied me and in a few minutes there was a knock on my door. When I opened it Billy said, "Well, here's my beloved Oral," and stuck out his hand. We shook and I invited him in.

In the room Billy began to tell of the great results he had seen of my work in Australia. I was listening but not responding. It hurt me down deep that the media had built him up as an honest man and me as a dishonest man.

While he was talking, I just blurted out, "Billy, you've never seen the day when you were more honest than I am."

He was taken aback, but he sensed that I was laboring inside. He replied gently, "Oral, I know that."

I didn't stop. I said, "Every article about you is about how honest you are and the great work you're doing. Everything said about me is the opposite. My ministry is vilified. I'm painted as a villain and my ministry is ridiculed. But, Billy, I want you to know my office and my life are conducted in the highest ethical manner."

Billy said something then that broke me up. He said, "Oral, I went to Australia and was praised. You went and were persecuted. I had a great press in the country and you didn't. But I want you to know something. I have my problems. They are just as serious to me as yours are to you. They are just as hurtful."

That bowled me over. He then went on to underscore how much he appreciated my ministry. His words could not have come at a more opportune moment.

It was a critical time in my ministry. Every man at some time in his life has self-doubts. I would be dishonest to say I haven't. Sometimes I have finished a crusade so completely exhausted that I could hardly bear to think of facing another sick person. I had given everything I had, preached as best I knew, prayed as faithfully as I could.

Then I would pick up a newspaper and read a story on the crusade from a reporter who had never even talked to me or bothered to check the truth of his facts. He would make wild charges and accusations so patently false that it was unbelievable to me that his editor would print them. In those moments self-doubt would sometimes wash over me. And I would wonder if it were really worth it.

In Australia I had had the worst imaginable press. I was ridiculed unbelievably. I couldn't understand why. Then when I saw the warm reception Billy Graham, the only other evangelist in the world with as large or larger an outreach as our ministry had, it was more difficult to understand.

Billy had begun his evangelistic ministry about the same time as I had. He had known the pressure and demands that come from being a well-known public figure. And he had remained close to God and kept a sensitivity to the needs of people.

There was no man in the world who could have ministered Christ to me then as did Billy. His was a word I needed desperately to hear.

It was about this time that attendance at both of our public meetings began to peak. Billy was in New York at

Madison Square Garden and I was in Trenton, New Jersey, at the same time. Both of these were the largest stateside meetings either of us had ever conducted.

Since that time we have maintained a warm relationship. There have been many occasions for us either to get together personally or to correspond. At Billy's invitation in 1966 I attended the Berlin Congress on Evangelism of which he was honorary chairman.

Dr. Carl H. Henry, who was then editor of *Christianity Today* magazine, had sent me an invitation and relayed to me Billy's personal wish that I would attend.

It was a difficult decision to make. It meant canceling a crusade, as well as a seminar, and also being absent at a critically important time at the University. However, after much consideration and prayer, I decided to go. A member of the ORU faculty, Dr. R. O. Corvin, accompanied me.

Dr. Corvin commented several times about the response of the delegates to my being there. Although he had impressive academic qualifications, Dr. Corvin had been raised on a farm. He used a farm boy analogy to explain it. He said, "Oral, as a boy, when we brought a new animal to the farm, the other farm animals would 'eye' him for some time.

"Your presence at the Congress was like that. Every room we entered people turned and looked, whether it was the convention hall, the lunch room, or the hotel lobby."

I knew what he meant, for I was aware that many delegates to the Congress considered my ministry of

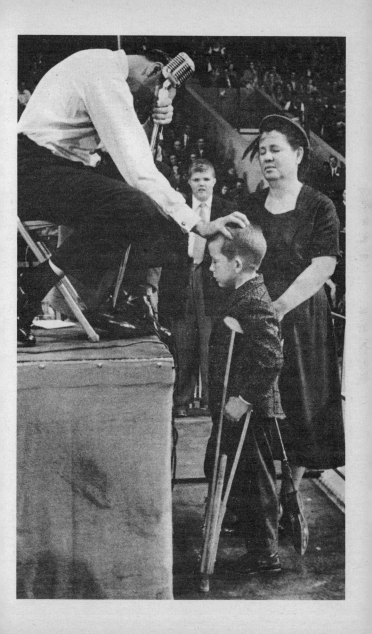

9. Oral Roberts with Masai tribesmen in Africa . . .

10. . . . with former Prime Minister David Ben-Gurion on visit to the Holy Land.

11. . . . and in Vietnam.

12. Praying with Mahalia Jackson on an Oral Roberts television spectacular.

13. Dick Ross, Oral Roberts, and Richard Roberts at TV studio in California.

14. Senator Mark Hatfield was a guest on television special.

15. The $30,000,000 campus of Oral Roberts University.

16. With Billy Graham at dedication of Oral Roberts University.

17. The Prayer Tower, a 200-foot steel and glass spire at center of campus is the home of KORU-FM, a 100,000-watt radio station, and the Abundant Life Prayer Group, a telephone counseling service.

evangelism and healing to be on the periphery of the great stream of evangelical Christianity.

I had been asked by Billy and Dr. Henry to chair a panel on twentieth-century evangelism. Every seat in the room was taken and there was no standing room left. The overflow was so great that people had to be turned away.

The questions were lively and interesting. Before the session was over I felt a new attitude emanating from those present. They must have been helped, for from that moment on I was stopped everywhere I went for advice and suggestions.

One man from India I remember in particular told about being asked to pray for a little boy who was dying. The boy was healed. But this minister had never prayed for anyone before and he was still disturbed about it.

When he told me of the incident he asked, "Brother Roberts, I came here to ask you this question: did I do right?"

The Holy Spirit gave me the answer, "Why don't you ask the little boy?"

Soon it seemed that everybody at the Congress had heard my response, "Ask the little boy."

Around the close of the Congress Billy presented me to the Congress:

Our prayer is going to be led by a man that I have come to love and appreciate in the ministry of evangelism. He has just built, and is in the process of building, a great university. He is known throughout the world through his radio and his television work, and millions of people listen to him. They read what he writes and they thank God for his ministry. I am speaking of Dr. Oral Roberts, and I'm going to ask him to say a word of greeting to us before he leads the prayer.

My remarks were brief but sincere. I said:

If there is a phrase that characterizes this Congress to me it is "we have been conquered by love." I could not conceive in advance what God would do in my heart as I found that men of diverse backgrounds, religious persuasions, and beliefs could not only sit together, but could learn to understand each other.

I shall always be glad that I came. When I left I was tense—tense from the problems of a growing ministry. I needed to sit down and listen to someone else for a change.

I thank you, Billy, and Dr. Henry for helping to open my eyes to the mainstream of Christianity, and to bring me a little closer to my Lord.

I am concerned that we will be able to carry this home with us—that we will sit down and worship together, read the Bible together, pray together, and win souls together. And that we will never look at each other again as we have done in the past, but as one family through our Lord Jesus Christ.

Thank you, Dr. Billy Graham and Dr. Henry. I have learned so much.

I then prayed. Though it was only a short prayer, many people commented upon it. Several days before I had begun to feel a special burden for Billy's safety. In my prayer before the Congress I made mention of it.

Let us pray. We come to you, our Heavenly Father, not in our name, and not in our strength, but in the incomparable name of your Son, Jesus Christ of

Nazareth. We know that you scooped out the bed
for the oceans, flung the stars from your fingertips,
sculptured the mountains and hung the earth on
nothing. But that didn't save us. That didn't meet
our needs. It was your shed blood—your death. Your
breaking asunder the bonds of death, your standing
where the stone was rolled away, and looking over
the world and saying to your people, "Because I live,
ye shall live also."

We think of when you vaulted into space and rode
on the wings of the morning in your ascension. We
are grateful that when you arrived, you prayed to
the Father and He sent us the Paraclete, the Holy
Ghost.

We are thankful that you called the Apostles, and
they went forth in your tradition—men of faith, men
of compassion, men of miracles. But not only did
you do it for them, but you did it for us. We have
felt a response this week and, we pray that we shall
not lose it, but that we will find it increasing and
multiplying by your hands on us even as you multiplied the loaves and the fishes.

God, be merciful to us and help us for we need
you and want you, and we are determined that we
shall have you.

God, bless the wives who are back home and our
children and the people we represent.

And, God, bless Billy and protect him. Satan, we
adjure you in the name of Jesus Christ, whose we
are and whom we serve, you shall not touch this
man, God's servant. And we ask you, Lord, to anoint
him as he has never known it before, but that he shall
speak with a new force, a new power, a new vision
to this whole generation.

Bless his team, this dedicated group of men, and
let them feel our love and appreciation.

May tonight, and tomorrow, and the closing service on Friday, be for your glory, the glory of your only begotten Son because He will invade this place and He will speak to us, and we will say, "Speak, Lord, for Thy servant heareth Thee." We ask in the name of Christ. Amen.

After the Congress was over we heard the news that the plane in which Billy had flown to London had been in danger but had landed safely. One of the delegates traveling with Dr. Corvin and me turned and said, "Brother Roberts, that's an answer to prayer."

The Congress was an exceptionally meaningful one for me, for I discovered a warmth and response to my ministry from leaders in the religious world that was most encouraging. In fact, many of them publicly witnessed to their affirmation of the ministry of healing. Had it not been for this meeting it would have been much more difficult for me to understand God's directing me to transfer my ordination to the Methodist Church in 1968.

There have been other times we've met since then, too. Billy was the dedicatory speaker for Oral Roberts University in 1967. Several times we have discussed the differences in our television ministry. I have felt a continuing personal affirmation from Billy Graham that I deeply appreciate. In my opinion, he is God's man for a special ministry to the nation. He stands in a unique role as spiritual leader for many of the nation's and the world's top echelons. He has never compromised his message. Success has only sharpened his witness. God continues to use him mightily. God bless Billy Graham, my good friend.

CHAPTER 10

Return to the Methodist Church

In 1947 as I was experiencing some of my earliest responses to this ministry a man came to our home and asked to visit with me. He said he was from the Methodist Church and he was there to request me to bring my ministry into Methodism. That really surprised me, for I didn't know any officials in Methodism were even aware I existed.

We visited awhile and finally I told him it was most flattering to receive such an invitation, but I had no feeling from God that I should take such a step at that time. And if it were not God's time, then it would be wrong to try and force it.

Little did I know that twenty years later I would join the Methodist Church and that doing so would come nearer closing this ministry down than anything in its history.

Had I known the furor it would cause I might have

been tempted never to take the step. I had behind me twenty years of a successful ministry, a university bore my name, and there was growing respect for the ministry of healing throughout the nation.

Yet joining the Methodist Church was a step that I had been wrestling with for some time. Really, "joining" is not the right word, for the first church I ever belonged to was the Methodist Church.

My grandfather had been a steward in the former Methodist Episcopal Church South and it was the first church my parents belonged to.

Another link with Methodism was a very close friendship I had with the late Dr. Forney Hutchinson, pastor of one of Methodism's largest churches. He had been a close friend of mine while I was pastoring in Shawnee, Oklahoma, in the mid-forties. We met at Bob McLaughlin's barbershop.

Dr. Hutchinson told me that Bob always cut ministers' hair free. I had never accepted such gifts, feeling that the salary paid me by my church entitled me to pay my way. When Bob refused my money, I insisted and explained my reasons. He was greatly impressed and so was Dr. Hutchinson.

Dr. Hutchinson took a personal interest in me, often coming by our house and encouraging me. He gave me the thought about the "Fourth Man" in the book of Daniel in the Old Testament which I later developed into a sermon that is my best known. Years later when I moved to Tulsa, Dr. Hutchinson had returned there to retire. He had been pastor of the Boston Avenue Methodist Church in Tulsa and was greatly beloved by Tulsans. Just before his death he came to see me and asked me to lay hands on him in prayer and benediction. I was in my early thirties and he was in his seventies. He couldn't see very well at that time, but his spiritual discernment was as sharp as ever. He said, "Son, when I met you in Shawnee the Lord drew me to you. I have only one word of advice: keep humble before Him and He will bless you and many more through you." I value the memory of his friendship and the fellowship we had in Christ.

In Tulsa it has always been my custom to visit different churches throughout the year. In this way I came to meet Dr. Finis Crutchfield, pastor of Boston Avenue United Methodist Church. Finis has a genuine Christian warmth and congeniality about him that awakens an immediate response in almost everyone who meets him. It was true for me also. And on one occasion when a national radio preacher began to attack ORU, Dr. Crutchfield defended both the University *and* its president.

Despite such friendships, I never thought too much of leaving the Pentecostal Holiness denomination to which I had belonged for over twenty-five years. Though it was one of America's smallest Pentecostal sects, I had never hesitated to identify with it.

In our crusades the ministers of the Pentecostal Holiness Church who cooperated in our meetings were always introduced, and I encouraged the people to attend their church.

Admittedly, there was a mixed response on both our parts. My own work had grown to such size that my rela-

tionship with them was incongruous. When I tried to contribute a sizable personal gift to help them move their
headquarters from a little 'town in Georgia of less than
five hundred people to Memphis, Tennessee, they declined. A friend of mine had volunteered a like amount.
Both were refused. It was almost as if they resented
success.

Yet I had very warm relationships with most of the
ministers and people. I continued to contribute to their
work and outreach.

My ministry, though, was never relegated to the Pentecostal Holiness Church or to Pentecostals. One night in
Columbus, Ohio, we took a written survey and there were
people from 122 different denominations present.

But as our work began to spread and grow I realized
that more Methodists responded positively to this ministry
than any other group. Their enthusiasm for our work
greatly encouraged me.

Perhaps it was while the foundations were being laid
for ORU that I began to sense for the first time that my
denominational affiliation was more important than I had
realized. For me the church has always been more than
a building or a certain group of organized people, much
less a name.

Yet as the University began to take form, I began to
see the possibility of others unwittingly taking it down
the denominational trail. When I considered how much
more likely this could be after my death, I began to have
serious questions.

Let me explain more fully. That which distinguishes

Pentecostal groups from other churches is not their organization or the name of their church. Rather, it is that at the turn of the century the founders of the Pentecostal churches reclaimed a valid Biblical experience—the Baptism with the Holy Spirit and speaking in tongues. It is called the Pentecostal experience.

Most of these early leaders were members of the historic churches. Yet opposition to speaking in tongues was such—and there were many misuses of it—that "tongue-talkers" were uniformly removed from the church rolls.

This brought about the founding of numerous Pentecostal churches such as the Assemblies of God, the Church of God (Cleveland, Tennessee), the Pentecostal Holiness Church and others.

Speaking in tongues became a badge of identification. Anyone who spoke in tongues sooner or later gravitated to one of the Pentecostal denominations.

However, in the forties and fifties when the impact of my ministry began to reach into other denominations, many people began to affirm not only the healing ministry, but the ministry of the Holy Spirit, which included speaking in tongues. Very few of them saw any need for leaving their own churches. Too, many churches had become more open to such diversity which made it more simple to remain.

A gradual division between these *new* Holy Spirit people and those of the institutional Pentecostal denominations occurred. The Pentecostal denominations felt if people really believed in the ministry of the Holy Spirit, they must make their witness to prove it by leaving their church and joining a Pentecostal denomination.

Other organizations developed such as the Full Gospel Businessmen's Fellowship, which is a group of dedicated laymen who affirmed that the baptism with the Holy Spirit and speaking in tongues was not a denomination, it was an experience. I urged my warm friend Demos Shakarian to start this group and was their first speaker. Thousands of sincere Christians began to respond to their witness and stayed in their churches to testify to others.

But at ORU, I began to discover, unfortunately, that there were many who held on to the belief that tongues was a badge of identification and people who believed in it should be channeled into the Pentecostal denominations.

The first real demonstration of my fears came about in relation to our seminary at ORU. I had never attended seminary myself and had never been totally convinced that America needed another one. But I had been persuaded that it was one way to train young men in the concepts of this ministry.

Such training never happened. When representatives from the seminary went to Chile in advance of my crusade there, I later discovered that the leader of the delegation met with a Chilean Pentecostal denomination and arranged a merger between their denomination and his —all at the expense of ORU and eventually to the detriment of our crusade there.

When I lectured on evangelism in the seminary, I found little response to the concerns that had given birth to this ministry. Denominational tags, however, were very important.

I saw more and more that ORU had to maintain even

after my death its unique understanding of the "charismatic" ministry and never succumb to being a purely denominational school.

I began to feel that God was leading me to transfer to the Methodist Church. To my mind, the Methodist Church was more than a denomination. It represented all the diverse elements of historic Christianity. In its membership and ministry were deeply committed evangelicals. Yet it had radical liberals, too. More importantly, it had maintained a free pulpit; Methodist ministers could preach their convictions.

In the fall of 1966 while visiting with a Methodist minister friend of mine, I broached the subject and mentioned in passing that I had considered transferring to the Methodist Church. He didn't take me seriously.

Later that year I attended the Berlin Congress of Evangelism. There was a tremendous response from many denominational leaders to the healing ministry. It was a radical departure from similar gatherings in years past.

I've often felt the Lord had me go to Berlin so that I could see the openness in the historic denominations to this ministry.

The feeling that I should make a move kept coming to me. It was heightened by the fact that a good number of our faculty at ORU, including the executive vice-president, were Methodists. My chaplain and others were Methodist ministers. This was not something we had planned. We had sought the ablest and most dedicated man for the position. It had just happened this way.

In December 1967, Dr. Finis Crutchfield was with me

in a ministers' meeting and without any warning he said, "Oral, why don't you join the Methodist Church?"

I was caught off guard since that was the very same question I was privately wrestling with. To hear someone say it out loud startled me.

I passed off his comment without outwardly giving it much consideration. But I kept having strong leadings as the days went by that I should indeed rejoin the Methodist Church.

When making decisions such as these I've always been something of a loner. Many people, when facing crucial decisions, will call in their friends and trusted advisers. They will weigh the pros and cons and then make a decision that seems to be the best one available.

In the normal conduct of the affairs of my ministry I've always operated this way, too. But when it comes to crucial decisions I have seldom talked to anyone about the decision to be made.

In matters of this kind, the most important thing to me has always been the will of God. What did God want me to do? If it were God's will, I didn't have to worry about success or failure. God would see it through.

Perhaps that's why my decision was such a shock to the staff at the Evangelistic Association and to the faculty and students at ORU. There had been no advance warning of any kind.

During this time an associate of mine visited with Finis, and the matter of my joining the Methodist Church came up. Finis then, on his own, arranged a meeting with Bishop W. Angie Smith, bishop of the Oklahoma–New Mexico Area, and invited me to it. When we met, Bishop

Smith told me that he had received several letters from ministers in the conference encouraging him to find out if I would join the Methodist Church. I was never more surprised. Only the week before he had received several telephone calls from pastors, including one district superintendent, indicating their burden for spiritual renewal in the church and expressing their opinion that Oral Roberts was the man who could help spark this.

I felt all of this was a further confirmation of that which I had been experiencing. After much prayer and serious heart-searching I decided to take the step.

Once again, though, in a meeting with Bishop Smith I queried him to make sure we understood each other.

I said, "Bishop Smith, you know I speak in tongues and pray for the healing of the sick."

"Yes, Dr. Roberts," he replied, "you can rest assured that I do know this."

"And you will take me as I am?" I asked.

"Yes, and if you changed we wouldn't want you!"

That was what I needed to hear. He went on to assure me that the only thing he was interested in was the saving grace of Jesus Christ. I made my final decision.

He and I had both agreed that we would not make a big production out of this. It was to be a private decision of one man and not a merger or uniting of movements.

Except for my wife and children, I shared this decision with only three people. The first was my mother. She and I have always been exceptionally close, particularly in spiritual matters. She was enthusiastically for it. The other two were Bob and Charlotte DeWeese. Bob had been my right-hand man as associate evangelist. He, better than any other, knew me and what this ministry stood for. Since 1951 he had been by my side as we ministered to millions of needy people throughout the world. I had absolute confidence in his integrity and commitment to Christ. Bob said, "Oral, besides your feeling that God wants you to do it, the structure of the Methodist Church will allow you the freedom you've wanted these nearly twenty years I've been with you. We're with you all the way."

But no sooner had word leaked out than rumors began to fly thick and fast. My staff at the Evangelistic Association, some of the faculty, and students at ORU, regents and partners began to bombard me with questions.

Outsiders picked it up and soon radio preachers low on material zeroed in on me. I was charged with having gone liberal, turning Communist, and being a backslider. They claimed inside information that I had made a deal to become a bishop, and in return ORU would belong to the Methodist Church. Nothing was further from the truth.

Close associates on my staff who were Methodist were either blamed or given the credit for my decision. No one could believe that it was a decision I had reached after long and careful deliberation and one which I felt was God's will for me.

On April 7, 1968, I joined Boston Avenue Methodist Church. The services of Boston Avenue Church were being regularly televised and that morning before a packed house and the television audience Dr. Crutchfield, in receiving me into the church, said, "Now I want to make this very clear. Dr. Oral Roberts is not joining the Methodist Church because he has changed his ministry. He is the same man with the same love for God and people. He belongs to all people because of his compassion and faith. We in this church fully understand this. I have prayed for this day to happen and I could not be happier."

I had not asked Finis to say that, but I was deeply grateful.

By May 1, all the appropriate forms and materials for transfer of my ministerial orders had been turned in. On May 24, I attended the Annual Conference in Oklahoma City and appeared before the conference. My membership was voted on by all the eligible ministers of the entire conference. I received a unanimous acceptance.

The very first church to which I was invited to speak following this was the black Wesley Methodist Church in Tulsa. After my sermon, they asked me to pray for them by the laying on of hands. It was a moving experience. Several wrote to tell me they had received help.

I shall always be grateful to Bishop Smith, who is now retired, for his gracious reception. He endured much opposition and criticism for it. We stood together until it was all proved wrong. We had always been in complete agreement regarding my new relationship. He knew as I did that I did not join the Methodist Church to receive but to give—of my time, my ministry, and myself.

For a long period due to my heavy schedule, I declined most invitations to speak in Methodist churches. Later, though, I began to accept a few. These have included some of America's largest pulpits and outstanding pastors such as Dr. Chess Lovern, Dr. Charles Allen, Dr. Lawrence Lacour, and of course, Dr. Crutchfield. I have spoken to national and regional meetings, and, at the invitation of bishops such as Earl Hunt, Kenneth Goodson and Lloyd Wicke, to their respective conferences. There is a mutual reciprocity that is open and strong.

And in 1970, at the invitation of Westminster Methodist Central Hall and with the support of the British Methodist Church, I conducted a week-long mission in London. My warm friend, Lord Rank, was a gracious host.

But the opposition sparked outside of Methodism is still hard to understand even in retrospect.

The intensity of it and the bitterness of many was far and above anything I had imagined. And the difficult part of it is that most of it came from men whom I had counted as my close friends. A lot of it was from men and leaders in the church to which I had formerly belonged.

As a young preacher boy I had left the Methodist Church and joined the Pentecostal Holiness Church. One of the things that attracted me to this denomination was their concern for the sick and for the individual. There was a spontaneity about their meetings and a love for people that reached me as a young man and made me wish to be part of them.

After I married I began to work very hard in the denominational structure. I helped create a small college in Oklahoma City, the first for the denomination to succeed west of the Mississippi. I also taught a couple of courses in religious education in the school for a while and was actively engaged in pastoring several churches. Thus, when I received letters of vilification from men I had grown up with and known so closely, it was a shock to say the least.

Each letter I received I answered personally by hand. As I had done through all the years when misunderstanding or opposition arose I never reacted in kind. I asked for their prayers and assured them of my love for them and my continuing commitment to the call God had placed on my life.

I also began to receive letters from partners and friends of the ministry who had supported our work through the years. It was with them that the most serious crisis came. For one thing the bad publicity did was to call into question the whole thrust of this ministry. People began to wonder if I had changed, if I still believed in healing, if I believed in prayers for the sick. If they wrote me would I still pray for them?

And so in the succeeding months, between the time I joined Boston Avenue in April and December of that year, our income at Oral Roberts University and our Evangelistic Association decreased by more than one-third. In fact, in those eight months it was necessary for my associates to go to the bank twice and borrow money to pay the several hundred employees on our payroll.

This was a difficult time for me. I'd made the change to the Methodist Church because I felt God willed it. A lot of people offered different reasons why I did it. But I knew deep down that my only reason was because I felt it was God's will for me.

In this time of crisis I was pushed back to the roots of this ministry. I even said to some of my associates, "If everything goes under, I'm ready to take my Bible, walk out, lock the door, and start all over."

I hoped that wouldn't happen but I was ready to do it without any question whatsoever. As I searched my life I began to feel that one of the causes of my problem was that I had allowed myself to become concerned about my own needs and not the needs of people. I had become concerned about whether or not Oral Roberts University would make it, whether the Evangelistic Association would make it, whether all of the offices overseas, the magazine, the printing, the radio and television programs would go on and not about the people whom I was trying to reach and minister to. In this time of reflection I began to restudy the Bible, and as I did the principles which I now call Seed-Faith began to come alive for me in a new way.

I told about this in the following sermon given recently in Winston-Salem, North Carolina. Nearly two thousand laymen and preachers from the Western North Carolina Conference, one of Methodism's largest, gathered for a day on "Seed-Faith." This is what I said:

> Twenty-four hours a day at the Abundant Life Prayer Group on our campus at ORU telephone calls come in from around the world. Over 150,000 a year call in for prayer regarding their needs. Each day I am given a report of who called and what their need is.
>
> In addition to this I receive a large volume of mail from men and women writing me for prayer. Their needs are indescribably serious. I've discovered that people will write you of deep needs that they could never tell you about in person.

Because of my mail and the calls that come to the Abundant Life Prayer Group I am provided an unusually accurate barometer of where people are hurting the most. Not too long ago I kept a log of the different problems and needs they had. There are four most common.

The largest number comes from people in need of spiritual and physical healing, either for themselves, or loved ones; and sometimes both.

The next largest number is surprising—it is for financial needs to be met. They say, "My bills are piling up and I have little money to pay with," or "My debts are overwhelming me," or "My salary is too small, I can't feed my family." In the most prosperous nation on earth it's staggering to see how many people are in serious financial trouble.

Loneliness is next. It seems everybody is lonely in some way. It's a big country, people live close to each other but the distance of concern and love is often like a thousand miles or more. I hear this from the old and the young, married and unmarried. It's an eye-opener to the real needs of people.

The fourth largest is actually a category I call "trouble." This is a word people use to designate problems in the home, in the marriage, with children or parents, with in-laws, with the church, etc.

Someone once said, "Everybody has a problem, or he is a problem, or he lives with one." This is literally true of all of us from time to time. Also, it seems that when one problem is solved, another takes its place.

I'm convinced more firmly than ever that the only way a person can be helped is when he has a need and recognizes that he does. If this ministry has tried to do anything it is always to be aware of the needs of people for that's what the Gospel is all about.

Jesus came to meet needs. He is where the need is. That's where to look for Him. He's there in the form of that need, to meet it.

Knowing this is what stimulates me to keep going. For when I help a person get his needs met, somehow it comes back to me in the answer of one of my own needs.

I remember going to church one Sunday morning and the minister opened the service by saying, "We're now in God's house. Let us lay aside our problems and worship the Lord."

I thought, "Oh, God, how I wish I were out of here." For instead of ministering to meet the needs of people he saw the service as an escape from the reality of a need-filled individual.

Jesus though came to meet the problem. He said, "I am come that you might have life and have it more abundantly." He identified with the halt and the lame, the sick and the oppressed, the outcast and forgotten. His life was consumed in meeting the needs of the people.

By His life He demonstrated that needs exist to be met. Whether it was a need for bread or wine, money or fish, healing, encouragement, guidance, salvation, He met those needs. In Christ, needs exist to be met. The principles of Seed-Faith help me to understand how Christ continues to meet a person's need in the now.

The first key principle of Seed-Faith is that God is your *Source*. One of the many scriptures that has impressed me very much as I've read the Bible has been Philippians 4:19: "For my God shall supply all your needs according to his riches in glory, by Christ Jesus." God is your supply!

A young man on our Board of Regents at ORU

flew to Tulsa some time back to visit with me. He sat down and poured out his heart. He was a builder, but tight money had struck and his loan sources had dried up. He had over one hundred men on his payroll, and he didn't know whether to discharge them or keep them on. Yet he knew if he kept them on he'd soon be bankrupt. He couldn't build because he couldn't borrow. He was beside himself. He felt hostility and anger at his bank and the insurance companies. He was angry with himself for getting in this position. In fact, when he came out to see me he was angry at the whole world.

As we talked I said to him, "Jack, I've just written a book entitled *Seed-Faith*. It's not off the press yet, but here's a typed copy. Go over to one of the dorm rooms and read it, then come back and see me."

He read it completely through, finishing about four in the morning. He picked up the phone after he finished it, called his wife and said, "Honey, everything's okay now."

She asked, "Jack, did you get a loan out there?"

He answered, "No. I found out Who my source is."

Later he explained to me. "I had been mad at the bank and mad at the insurance companies for not lending me money. I was looking to them as sources, not instruments. As a Christian I have only one source—God!"

As he said that, I thought to myself the reason that particular part of my book had impressed him so is because I too had gone through the same struggle. During the financial crisis following my joining the Methodist Church I can still remember the shock I received when it dawned on me that I was not thinking of God as my source.

When I analyzed my own condition I realized that

I was beginning to think of people as my source. Inadvertantly, I was looking to people to pay the bills. I was depending on people to help us take the steps of faith we needed to take. I decided then and there that first I was once again going to claim God as my source and if the instruments He used were faithful and helped us, fine. If not, I would still depend on God.

That insight began to permeate my thinking. I began to develop a whole new attitude toward the problems we were facing. And because I was no longer so anxious and frustrated, I could begin to think creatively about solutions.

I found that relationships with my associates at the office began to take on a new dimension. They had felt some of the same pressures and I had perhaps even intensified them. When I began to talk about this principle I could almost see them breathe deeper! For they recognized its rightness. God was our source; it was God who would supply our needs.

But that was only a partial insight. There was more to discover.

It happened that about this time we were trying to sell a large piece of equipment. It had served its purpose but it was outdated and needed to be replaced. A small evangelistic association had expressed interest in it. I did not know these men and had never heard of their work, but when I was introduced to them, I felt a sincerity about them and wanted to help them.

God spoke in my heart: "Don't sell them this equipment. Give it to them." When I mentioned this to my associates, and our financial counsel, they were against it. Here we were suffering our worst monetary crisis in the entire twenty years of our ministry.

Debts were piling up, we had to borrow money to make the payroll, and I was talking about giving something away when we desperately needed the funds from its sale.

It was then that the second key principle of Seed-Faith came into being for this problem. It's best expressed in Luke 6:38, where Christ teaches, "Give, and it shall be given unto you."

Somehow I felt that part of the future of our ministry hinged on whether or not we as a ministry dramatically symbolized that we took this principle seriously. I had been doing it personally. Would we now do it corporately? As my associates and I discussed it and I shared my feelings, they began to respond positively. In fact, they eventually encouraged me to authorize the gift.

It was a great feeling, for not only had we concluded that we were going to depend on God as our source, we had all agreed to give. Our whole attitude changed to one of giving. We began to seek ways we could better minister to the people and give more meaningfully.

The more I've studied this principle, the more convinced I am of its rightness. It is the great new focus Jesus brought in the New Testament which makes faith in Him relevant to the needs we face in the now. In the Old Testament giving was portrayed as an act of obedience, duty or loyalty. It was a debt one owed to God. One-tenth of income, one-seventh of time were owed to God.

But, in the New Testament, if you are a *follower* of Christ, giving is no longer a debt you owe, but a seed you sow! It does not diminish or impoverish you; rather, it is the source of your strength, your power, your wealth, your joy. It is in giving that you receive.

Under the Law of the Old Testament you received first, then from it you gave. In the New Testament you give first, and from what you give, it is given to you. It's a 180-degree shift.

For only what you give can God multiply, not what you receive. For example, when feeding the five thousand Jesus took the fish and the loaves the little lad *first* gave to Him and then blessed and multiplied them for the huge crowd. So in our lives we have to give something to God first before he can multiply it back to us.

In other words when you give, give as a seed you plant. In Galatians 6:7 the scripture states, "whatsoever a man soweth, that shall he also reap." And in verse 9 of that same chapter, "Let us not be weary in well-doing: for in due season we shall reap, if we faint not." In Matthew 17:20 Jesus said, "If you have faith as a . . . seed, you can say to the mountain, be thou removed, and it will obey you."

Giving is like sowing seed which introduces the third principle of Seed-Faith, "Expect a Miracle."

Nothing happens unto itself. For every cause there is a result. It's a false religiousness that expects nothing for something.

The farmer who plants his crops expects a miracle to result. The harvest is the miracle of his Seed-Faith. The law of sowing and reaping is God's multiplying back what you give. I call this a miracle.

Whatever you give—time, talent, love, compassion, money—it is the giving of yourself. God accepts it as Seed-Faith and multiplies it back to you.

A student on our campus complained to me that she had no time. There were so many things to do, and the day was not long enough to do them. My suggestion on how she might solve that problem really caught her off guard. I said, "Find someone who needs help and give them fifteen minutes a day of your time. And when you give it, do it as a seed you plant and expect God to multiply back what you need most—time."

I saw her sometime later and discovered she had taken my advice. Not only did she have adequate time now, she was holding down a part-time job as a tour guide for the campus. She said, "It's a miracle."

I mentioned earlier the piece of equipment we gave away. The very next month, January, we had our first upturn in income in eight months. In my opinion, one of the reasons for that response is not only that God came to our rescue, but I believe that this gift turned our eyes away from our own problems and made us start thinking of someone else's problems. Instead of thinking how we could sell something to help ourselves, we began to think how we could help someone else who had a need.

This whole idea began to go through our organization. The men on our staff began to get hold of it and to express it and share it. A new feeling of confidence and enthusiasm began to go through the whole ministry. Some of our men were literally transformed. They began to take on new responsibilities and to have a sense of consecration and dedication that was inspiring to behold. They once again realized that our very reason for existence was to meet the needs of people.

Instead of tapering off, response to the ministry began to grow as never before. Support for our outreaches doubled in less than two years. It was a miracle!

It was a hard lesson to learn. Anything worthwhile seldom comes easy.

Now when I start any new project or expect help from any place, I first give something. I give it to God Who is my Source, and through Him I expect my needs to be met. In other words, I say to a person who has a need: Give God your best, and give it first. Then ask God for His best, and expect a miracle.

There was a warm response to this explanation of Seed-Faith. What I said has become for me a way of life. Through the experience of joining the Methodist Church I gained a new insight into meeting the needs of people that has helped thousands. The book, *Miracle of Seed-Faith,* has surpassed in circulation each of the more than forty books I had written in the previous twenty years. It has long since passed the million mark. Our ministry took on a renewed vigor and commitment to people. Though sometimes I have wondered why God led me to take the steps He directed, I am glad I took them. That's what expecting a miracle is all about.

CHAPTER 11

How I Am Paid

When I drove into Tulsa in 1947 my total assets were three hundred dollars' worth of furniture, a car I was paying for in installments, and twenty-five dollars in cash.

It was a bold move and I did not know whether or not we would succeed. I felt though that God had spoken to me and I was determined to be obedient. During those days, my wife Evelyn was a constant source of encouragement to me.

I had first met Evelyn in 1936. Evelyn told me that she wrote in her diary that night: "I sat by my future husband tonight." The meeting was for only a few moments in the orchestra at a camp meeting of our church denomination at Sulphur, Oklahoma. I rushed up to the platform, leaned over to the girl seated to my right and asked this brilliant question: "Is my hair combed? Do I look all right?"

That was our only meeting until two years later

when, after seeing each other for only one weekend, we became engaged. Four months later we were married.

A good woman has many virtues, among them the ability to see a man as she believes he can be. That night in 1936 in answer to my question about my hair, she answered, "Oh, yes, you look very nice." Years later when I asked her what she really felt like saying, she said, "When I saw you rushing up, tall, black-haired, with your tie not on quite straight, your hair looking like you had had an accident with the comb, and you sat down and asked me if your hair looked presentable, I thought, 'A few years from now, when you are my husband, you will look very nice!'"

I was nearly twenty-one, I had been preaching for four years, and I felt I needed a wife. I wanted a sincere, dependable, yet beautiful and talented girl who would grace a budding minister's home and be an asset to his ministry. Evelyn had left her home in Westville, Oklahoma, the year before my parents had accepted a pastorate there. She was attending college in Texas and teaching school. I became acquainted with her parents, and soon mutual friends began telling me about her and urging me to meet her. They described her as a good musician, an excellent cook and housekeeper, and as a woman who was even-tempered, gracious, and charming in every way. She had recently passed her twenty-first birthday and was doing well in her studies and her schoolteaching.

I remembered my casual meeting with her in the orchestra at the Sulphur camp meeting in 1936, so I wrote her and sent her a copy of a small book I had published, putting a personal inscription inside. She replied immediately, and we began a correspondence. Her handwriting was lovely and I enjoyed her letters, so I began making plans to go see her.

One day I wrote: "Who knows but you may be a preacher's wife someday?" She replied: "If you think that, you are fooled. I don't intend spending my life in a parsonage, raising a bunch of preacher's children." She was immediately sorry for that, and followed the letter with another containing an apology. But it crossed my answer, in which I had tartly replied: "Who said anything about you and me getting married? Good-bye."

Her letter of apology soothed my pride, so I wrote back and apologized, too. I had been saving my money for a long time, and now I purchased a little blue Chevrolet coupe and drove down with my mother to the Rio Grande Valley in Texas to see Evelyn. When I drove up to her school, it was recess time, and the children shouted, "Miss Evelyn! Your boyfriend is here!"

I sat in the back of the schoolroom while she finished her class. She was very calm outwardly, but later she said that her heart was pounding and she could scarcely keep her mind on the book she was reading to the class. Sitting there, listening to her fine voice and watching her conduct her class, I thought, "She is even more lovely than they told me."

That evening after dinner, we went back to the school where she played the piano for me. The other teachers told her the next day, "Well, Evelyn, he's nice looking and all that, but you don't want to marry a preacher!"

But my mother liked Evelyn immediately and encouraged me. Before I returned to Oklahoma, I had made up my mind and proposed to Evelyn. On my last day we went fishing on the Gulf of Mexico, but caught nothing except one another. On the way back I stopped my car on a sandbar to talk. Finally I put my arm around her and said, "Evelyn, my huge, happy, hilarious heart is throbbing tumultuously, tremendously, triumphantly, in a lasting, long-lived love for you. As I gaze into your beauteous, bounteous, beaming eyes, I am literally lost in a daring, delightful dream in which your fair, felicitous, fancy-filled face is ever present like a colossal, comprehensive constellation. Will you be my sweet, smiling, soulful, satisfied spouse?"

I had learned this as a boy, and intended to have a bit of fun before getting down to the serious matter of proposing. Evelyn replied, "Listen here, boy! If you're trying to propose to me, talk in the English language." I did it over again and was accepted, and we sealed it with a kiss.

Years later, I related this story in a sermon and quoted my proposal. After the service a little ten-year-old boy stopped me outside the tent and said, "Wait a minute, preacher."

"What do you want, son?"

He grinned and said, "Preacher, would you write that thing down for me?"

I proposed to Evelyn in September 1938, and we made plans to marry at the end of her school term the following June. I returned to my evangelistic travels, holding meetings in several different states, but my heart grew fonder and fonder of her and more and more lonely for her. I knew I loved her and I wanted her by my side. I did not see her for four months, but we wrote every day, and through our letters we came to know each other better. In November I began pressing her for a Christmas wedding. Finally she asked the school board for permission, promising to return and finish the school term that year.

We were married on Christmas Day in Papa's church in Westville with the church filled with her friends and mine. The Reverend Oscar Moore performed the ceremony. He is now one of the trustees of the Oral Roberts Association. I had to borrow twenty dollars from the bank for wedding expenses, and Oscar Moore cosigned my note at the bank for the loan. He made a round trip of two hundred miles to be present at the ceremony, and I had only five dollars left of my loan to give him for performing the ceremony. He was very gracious and philosophical about it, remarking facetiously, "That's all right, Oral. I will collect what she's worth to you someday."

Since 1938, each year at our Christmas anniversary, I have sent a gift to Oscar. Recently I asked him if he didn't think I had paid him in full. He smiled and replied, "That's up to you, young man. When you think you have reached the point of Evelyn's full value, you can stop."

"But she's growing in value every year!"

"That's bad?" he asked.

After our marriage, Evelyn returned to Texas to finish her school term and I to the evangelistic ministry. Although we were newlyweds and madly in love, we were together only one weekend during the next four months. Once I was so lonesome for her that I wrote her a

burning letter telling her how much I loved her and
missed her. The same day I had written a pastor my acceptance of his invitation to conduct a revival in his
church. Inadvertently, I put Evelyn's letter in the envelope addressed to this pastor and his letter in her envelope. Well, the pastor took one look and said, "This is
not my letter!" and quickly mailed it back to me. In the
meantime, Evelyn had opened her envelope and read:
"Dear Brother, In reply to your invitation . . ." and said,
"Oh no!" She knew my state of mind was pretty bad,
for me to get the two letters mixed. She wrote: "Honey,
if you say the word, I will resign my second school term
this minute and come to you."

I managed to survive, and when her term was over
she came to me in Oklahoma where I had accepted the
pastorate of a small church. I was expecting her on Sunday morning. My congregation understood why I kept
looking out the window. "His new wife's coming, you
know," they whispered to each other.

Her salary as a teacher had been exactly twice as much
as mine was as a preacher, but she cheerfully accepted
the change, assuring me that we would get along all right.

The ministry we were embarking on was more of a
change than either of us had bargained for. We were not
prepared for the demands that would be made upon
us.

In my very first meeting in Tulsa some miraculous healings occurred, and I immediately began to receive phone
calls from people all over the nation pleading with me to

come pray for one of their loved ones who was sick and dying.

When I explained that I was in a meeting and could not come they would then offer to pay my plane fare. Again, I would decline and try to assure them that I would be willing to pray over the phone. In desperation many would offer to borrow money to pay me if only I would come. They pleaded, they threatened, and then tried to bargain. There was no way I could explain to their satisfaction.

It was repugnant to me that people felt my willingness to pray was based on their ability to pay. And I know it was debilitating to them to be forced to try and bargain for the life of one they loved.

Shortly before I left the pastorate to begin this ministry I attended a meeting in Enid at which the sick were being prayed for. I was thrilled at what I saw. There was a real movement toward God, people were being saved and healed. I was eager to be ministering in the same way.

Then something happened that deeply repelled me . . . offering time. The preacher spent more time pleading for money than he had preaching the Gospel. It made me sick to my stomach.

I went home and told Evelyn that there was no way I could enter a healing ministry if that was part of it. My reaction was further intensified by two local businessmen who also attended the same services and proposed to underwrite my efforts if they could share in the profits.

When Evelyn saw that I was serious she began to try to convince me I was wrong.

She said, "Oral, you're almost ready to launch out and this is just a test to help you know for sure you've got what it takes regardless of criticism." The more she talked the more convinced I became.

"If you do what is right," she said, "God will bless you despite what some uninformed critics might say."

Yet it took some time before I could overcome the resentment I had developed because I was consumed with a passion to maintain a high standard of personal ethics and integrity. I believed if God had called me into this work He would take care of my needs without pleadings and taking advantage of people. I still feel the same.

I believe the Bible when it says, "The love of money is the root of all evil." Money is not the root of evil, but the *love* of it is. "Loving money" is placing it above everything else—above honesty, decency, respect, honor, service, faith, or love. In that sense, money could become one's god.

While I was growing up, I never knew much about money. Papa was a preacher. We children soon got the idea that the people felt if God would keep our father humble, they would keep him poor.

It is no wonder that we came to associate Christianity with poverty. It was not easy to look upon God as a loving being when your father had preached for a month and was able to bring home only a few dollars, not nearly enough to clothe and feed and shelter his family.

When I married and started my own family, during the

first twelve years, Evelyn and I and our first two children, Rebecca and Ronnie, didn't really live—we existed. My earliest pastorate paid ten dollars a week and my last one, twelve years later, paid fifty-five dollars a week. Evelyn and I were heavy givers in relation to our earnings. We never gave less than a tenth of our income and when there was a special need in the church we would sometimes give our entire week's check.

At one pastorate there was no parsonage. We were forced to live with member families of the church. None of them seemed interested in the church's purchasing a house. Finally, Evelyn told me, "The Bible says that a man must provide for his family. I can't continue to live like this and raise a family. I am taking the children to my mother until you are able to secure a place for us."

I went straight to the church board and asked if they wanted a pastor without his family. They went into action by giving me permission to raise a down payment for a parsonage.

Evelyn and I gave one whole week's salary to get things started. We didn't know how we would make it, but we felt that we had to do it. Shortly after that one man in the church who had not really been very active heard about our giving. It moved him so, he couldn't sleep. Around three in the morning he got up and came to the house in which we were staying and knocked on the door.

When my wife told me he was waiting, I went to him, and he said, "Brother Roberts, I heard about what you did with your week's salary and it got ahold of me. I make a lot more than you do, but I've been giving less. Here's four hundred dollars on that down payment."

I tried to tell him that wasn't the reason we had given. He said he understood, but he wanted to give it anyway. It was instances like that which helped me to have enough faith to take some of the larger steps down the road of faith.

As I mentioned earlier, when it came time to leave my pastorate in Enid and enter into world evangelism through the healing ministry, I put my faith to the test by securing a downtown auditorium for our first large public healing service. The test was whether or not God would supply the rental of the building without any undue pressure on me or the audience. God supplied the amount plus a few dollars over.

During the first Tulsa crusade, one offering was received each week for expenses, and one as a love offering for me personally. The expense offering was used to purchase stamps, stationery, and meet secretarial expenses. The personal offering was to support my family.

The people wanted to give for my personal support. Some even earmarked their gift for us. I remember when the first offering of three hundred dollars was received, it was like a fortune. We needed furniture, clothes, a car and so many other things.

As I began to expand, I became increasingly aware that I needed to be scrupulously responsible with my personal finances as well as the ministry's. If there was any hint of taking personal advantage of people in need, it would be a deep black mark on my work as well as my conscience.

The best way to do this, I felt, was to organize the
ministry so that others would share in the financial decisions. In July of 1948 I felt it best to incorporate into a
nonprofit religious organization. Evelyn and I had several
hundred dollars in a savings account . . . the first we had
ever had. We drew it out and gave it to the attorneys and
it became the nucleus for the ministry to be established
financially.

Absolute and final authority over all financial matters
was put into the hands of a board of trustees. These were
dedicated Christian businessmen who had not only an
effective Christian witness but good business sense as
well.

These men brought their skills to bear in guiding the
ministry and directing its resources meaningfully. Since
it was customary for evangelists in my denomination to
be paid by a love offering, their first recommendation was
that I live entirely from freewill offerings instead of a
salary. When we got down to deciding what this would
mean, I agreed to accept only one offering in each
crusade. Additionally, I reaffirmed that under no circumstances would I accept personal gifts from anyone
whether they were large or small. Gifts sent to me personally would automatically be turned over to the
Evangelistic Association for disbursement. I could not afford to allow people to equate healing prayers with
money. I have often offended people because I refused
the money they tried to put in my hand after I had
prayed for them. I had promised God I would not touch
the gold or the glory. I meant it.

In our crusades, when it came time to receive an offering its use and purpose was always explained. Sometimes it was to be applied to advertising, or transportation, or for follow-up work after the crusade had closed. It was always made clear that none of it would go to me personally.

Then on the very last night of the meeting a brief simple appeal would be made by the person in charge. "Tonight's offering will go in its entirety to Brother Roberts. Brother Roberts accepts no personal gifts for his prayers nor does he receive a salary from any outside source. You are invited tonight to share in his support." Then the ushers waited on the audience as the service continued.

Despite how hard some critics tried to discredit the practice, I never questioned the propriety of this arrangement. The reason was that I knew how much the offerings really were, and they fell far below the critics' estimate.

Because our crusade attracted a large number of the unchurched and the sick, the offerings were many times below the budget of expenses. Churchgoing people are simply much more accustomed to giving. Then, too, many of the sick were in desperate financial straits because of heavy medical expenses.

We continued on the love offering basis until about 1960. However, as the ministry grew I reached a point where I became uncomfortable receiving a love offering in each crusade. After much prayer I made a decision to go on salary.

By this time our assets had become substantial, although not anything like reported. However, it was large enough for me, a minister, to feel uncomfortable. It had been gained through incomparably hard work, through being at home an average of eight days a month and through helping people at the point of their need.

Our holdings consisted mainly of real estate. We never had much cash, for it had been our policy to give generously, pay our living expenses, and invest the rest by making a down payment on a piece of property and then paying the balance in installments.

In 1962, Evelyn and I divested ourselves of our holdings and gave the money to help Oral Roberts University get off the ground. I also made arrangements so that royalties from any books I wrote would go into a trust for my children, or directly to the University. I felt especially strong about providing some resources for my children because of the burden they had borne as a result of the misunderstanding of this ministry and my constantly being away from home.

My salary was set at fifteen thousand dollars a year with a home to be provided. In ten years I received two raises.

Shortly after I was elected president of ORU, responsibility for my salary was assumed by the University and set at twenty-four thousand five hundred dollars by the Board of Regents, which was made up of some forty men and women from across America. I now receive no remuneration whatever from my evangelistic work.

Not too long ago one of Tulsa's national banks elected me a director. Normally, such positions are held by men of personal wealth. Because of ORU's increasing significance in our community they felt it would be good busi-

ness for them and for us to have a representative of the
college on their board of directors.

Yet they also felt quite certain that I was personally
wealthy. When I turned in my certified financial statement, the bank's president could hardly believe it, for
much to his surprise, I lived on a salary with no substantial financial worth. He said, "People need to know
this." It was a witness I was proud to make.

CHAPTER 12

Tents: From the First to the Last

My first tent had a capacity of three thousand. When I first saw it erected, I wondered if I had not made a huge mistake. Would I ever fill anything that large? Would that many people ever come to hear a preacher from Oklahoma?

At the time it was the largest portable tent in use for the Gospel in America. It had taken a miracle of faith to get it all together. In fact, I could write an entire chapter on all the things I had to do to get it ready. At any rate, we were to begin our first crusade in June 1948.

I must confess, I am not mechanically minded and have never had any ability working with my hands. We set about erecting the tent, but I could not tell the men how to do it. I had been assured it would be a relatively simple matter when I purchased it, but to erect a tent 100 feet wide by 220 feet long is no simple operation. Space had been purchased in the local paper stating that the meeting would start on Thursday, but I was unable to get the tent up until Saturday.

A company had sold us some push-type poles that were supposed to make the tent go up easily. We started to push the canvas up and got it one-third the distance between the ground and the top of the poles. There the great mass of canvas hung. We pushed and tugged and lifted until we thought our backs would break. We stayed under the canvas so long that one man had to be carried out because of heat prostration. Dark was coming on that first evening and the tent was one-third in the air. That was as far as we could get it. I still remember climbing out from under the canvas and walking off by myself to try to figure out something to do.

My critics had said that we would never get the tent up. They said I would never hold a successful meeting in Durham, North Carolina. They said that my ministry wouldn't last. They had said a lot of other things. There I stood with the tent one-third up and with no hope that it would ever go any higher. I had spent all the money I had for expenses and all I had was personal money to feed my family and pay our rent at the motel until an offering was taken. It was less than a hundred dollars. Standing there under the flap of the tent, I felt more discouraged than ever before in my life. It seemed that I had come to a dead-end street. If I had had enough money, I could have sent for a man who knew how to erect tents. But I didn't have it. So I said out loud, "Lord, I don't know how in the world I'm going to do this, but I'm going to do it. I'm going to get this tent up. I am going to hold this revival."

I didn't know that a man had walked up behind me and was watching. He heard that prayer, and it touched him. The first thing I knew he was tapping me on the shoulder and saying, "Look here, preacher, you just quit that worrying. We are going to put this tent up."

He turned and walked away. Pretty soon I heard him call the men to come over to him. When I walked up, he was saying to them, "Men, I've got a little money. I'm going to hire some men. This preacher here has got something in his soul, and the Lord has sent him to us. I'm going to stand by him. How about you?"

A change came over the men. They began pulling out their billfolds and counting their money. The next morning they had located a tent man, and the work began to hum. By Saturday noon we had the new tent raised, the platform erected, the seats in place, and only one thing remained to be done.

One of the sponsoring pastors ran up and said the light company would not turn on the lights until I had put up a deposit of ninety-seven dollars. I looked at the big tent as it towered toward Heaven. One of the men nearby remarked that it looked like a giant tent cathedral. It was so big, so beautiful, so beyond anything I'd ever seen that a lump came into my throat. I thought to myself, "Lord, we finally got the tent up and everything is ready for the meeting. Now we don't have any lights. What am I going to do?"

I said, "Men, I'll be back in about an hour."

I drove quickly to the motel, went in and told Evelyn what had happened. I said, "Honey, give me a check. I have to have ninety-seven dollars to get the lights turned on in the tent."

She said, "Oral, that's all we have."

I said, "Write the check quick. We've got to get the lights on."

She said, "Okay. We'll either lose everything we have together or we'll come out on top together."

We did much praying and believing during those days wondering how the Lord would work everything out and help us pay all the bills, but the meeting was a great success.

From Durham on, the meetings continued to grow. Everywhere we went attendance increased. Soon it was necessary to purchase an even larger tent. Attendance kept growing. Many times it was not unusual for me to preach for more than two hours. (That is a miracle I myself have difficulty believing now.) Following my sermon, I would sometimes pray for hundreds of people. The services would last from three to four hours and still the response continued to grow.

Perhaps one of the more picturesque reports that captured the spirit of these crusades was a report on one of the crusades in the East in which a church editor wrote about the first time he attended one of my crusades.

The preacher said, "Please stand for the dismissal prayer." There was a mighty stir in the vast audience that packed the world's largest gospel tent.

While a sponsoring pastor came forward to pronounce the benediction, I glanced at my watch. It lacked just 20 minutes being 11 o'clock at night. I knew some of those people—hundreds of them in fact—had been on the meeting grounds since 2 o'clock in the afternoon. That meant that they had been present for more than nine hours for that one service. I knew also that thousands of them had driven for many miles to attend that service, some of them a hundred miles or more. They would return to their homes that night, and would be on their jobs the next morning at the usual hour. Knowing these things, I wondered what brought them here. Why do the people come like this? Why do they respond to this preacher like this?

And even as I asked myself the question, I smiled at my own naïveté. What was I doing there? My own home was nearly two hundred miles away. Yet, here I was. I, who chafed at delays, traffic jams, and shoving crowds, was tonight caught in the greatest traffic jam in this state.

While thinking of these things, I stood watching the vast lake suddenly burst through its banks and turn into a human river flowing below me, outward toward the highway or the parking lots. I estimated that if everything continued to move smoothly, I might get my car out of the jam within the next 45 minutes; and somehow I didn't feel at all rushed. That wasn't like me. Well, the only conclusion was, I had become a part of the thousands. I had come for one purpose, only one: to hear Oral Roberts preach and to see him in action!

I am a devotee of efficiency, and in matters pertaining to evangelism, this evangelist is efficiency embodied. From the moment the organist sounds the first note of a song there is not a hitch.

As Oral Roberts is introduced, thousands of people come to their feet when he almost literally glides to the front of the platform (there is no pulpit).

Thousands join him in a chorus. He sings a stanza solo and then the chorus again. This done, "Do you love Jesus tonight?" he asks.

"Amen!" the audience responds.

"With all your heart?"

"Amen!"

"Now," says the evangelist, "before you sit down, turn around and shake hands with three people near you, and say, 'Neighbor, God loves you.'" The response to this request is as universal and as enthusiastic as to any of the others he makes during his hours of action.

The Oral Roberts sermons are actually the high light of the meeting so far as I am concerned. I have been listening to sermons ever since I was a little boy. I have appreciated good sermons all my life. I enjoy a good sermon more than a good song. But with all that appreciation for great sermons, Oral Roberts is the only man on top of the earth who has ever held my attention for 2 hours and 15 minutes and then closed, leaving me wishing that he would go on! Why? You tell me!

His Scripture lessons are unusually long for an evangelist. No snappy sentence texts are used to catapult his sermons into a sensational, disjointed appeal to men's ignorance of the Scriptures. From the word go, he is a Bible preacher. The beginning of his messages is deliberate, sometimes almost slow. Here again, I have wondered how he holds the people through those introductions. He never talks above their heads. He talks to their eyes. He probes their hearts. He never leaves them for a somersault on the Milky Way. He is always down to earth. He never teases them with so-called double talk. They understand his language. He never bores them with theological hairsplitting. With him, salvation is being saved. Healing is being healed. Holiness is getting right and living right. Jesus is the Savior of the world. Our God is a good God, and the devil is a bad devil.

His critics accuse him of being top-heavy on the healing idea. What the man preaches is faith in God. He preaches the Book of Acts and the Four Gospels. The Four Gospels tell what Jesus began to do and to teach. The Book of Acts tells how the disciples followed up His work after His death, resurrection, and ascension. And this is the source of most of the Oral Roberts sermons.

His style of preaching is pointed and positive. Only a minimum of time is spent preaching against things. He preaches for something. With a man-size microphone in his hands, he walks over the platform, his eyes sweeping every angle, every square foot of the great tent. There is hardly a person there but who feels he has been preached to before the sermon is over.

Oral Roberts' voice is pleasant to listen to. It never takes the tone of harshness. Even when he raises it sharply it attracts rather than repels. Now his voice warns, now it cajoles, now it entreats, now it reaches out and seems almost to crackle like a bullwhip above the heads of the audience. But even the lash never quite descends to cut the people. Like the lash of a whip in the hands of an expert driver, it doesn't hurt the team; it merely spurs them to action.

His sermons are not sensational, but they are dramatic. He can assemble a group of people on the platform, put them through the paces of conversation and action, and make you see the thing he is talking about. His dramatic description of the dice game at the foot of the cross of Christ is an example of this. There is no cross there; there are no gambling soldiers there. And yet you see them all. Oral Roberts becomes the cross, the gamblers, the conversation. The characters come to life, and you see them clearly. He rarely uses descriptive phrases, and yet he makes you see. His words are words of action. Like a clever writer, he never wastes paper trying to describe a landscape. He simply carries you over the countryside and lets you see it for yourself. Perhaps this is why you do not tire of his 2-hour sermons. You forget that they are sermons at all. They become interesting excursions into a wonderful country that you have always wished you could have witnessed. Who would get tired of such interesting excursions in a brief two hours?

Now here is what he has been working on from the first second he stepped on the platform. You don't realize his sermon is finished when you first hear his, "Let every head be bowed, please." You get the idea that this is but a continuation of what he started out to do when he picked up his Bible to read the lesson. Ten thousand heads are bowed at his request. Then he prays:

"Dear God, grant me this miracle tonight, according to thy Word. Don't let a mother's boy, don't let a mother's girl, who has heard me preach tonight, go to hell. Don't let a mother, don't let a daddy, who has heard me preach tonight, go to hell." Then to the audience:

"Keep your heads down. Now listen, neighbors, if you will do exactly as I say, I can help you. But if you do not do exactly as I tell you, there is nothing I can do for you. I want every man, every woman, every boy, and every girl here, who believes in my prayers and wants my prayers, that you may find the forgiveness of God for your many sins and the peace of God for your lonely souls, to take the first step in Jesus' name, and raise your right hand.

Quickly, please, put your hands up and then take them down. Thank you. Now, you who have not yet raised your hands, and you want my prayers, put your hands up quickly and take them down. Thank you. Thank God!

"Please, everybody, keep your heads down. Now, listen to me, neighbor. Every one of you, without exception, who raised your hands take the second step in Jesus' name, and stand up on your feet! Stand up! That's right. Oh, thank God, they're getting up! Now, there are others who raised your hand and you have not stood up yet. If you do not stand up, I cannot help you; but if you will stand, I can help you back to God. Please stand!

"Now, all of you except those standing keep your heads down. You who are standing look on me. Friends, I am so glad you are standing, and I'll tell you why. This is God's night to set you free. Please do not sit back down! I have below me here a place where you may come and stand, and I will pray for you and help you back to God. Please take this third step in Jesus' name, and come right now. Oh, thank God, they're coming down every aisle! Now, lift your heads, neighbors, and see what God is doing."

I have given you this rather lengthy description of the Oral Roberts altar call that you may see the logical sequence of powerful steps employed by this master evangelist to get souls to God. And do they come? Since then, on two different occasions, I have seen as many as five thousand people respond in one night.

No matter how early they come to the service, comparatively few leave before the last person has "gone through the healing line." Perhaps in no other phase of his work is the evangelist criticized more severely or misrepresented more unjustly than in this. Yet, here he is his humblest self. He endears himself to tens of thousands of people by the smooth efficiency of his operation, the gentle touch that he gives God's suffering people, the irresistible attraction he has for little children, the bold challenge that he hurls into the devil's face every time he prays for a sick person.

I was astonished the first time I saw him take his place in the chair at the head of the healing line. He started his activities something like this, "Before I pray for the sick tonight, I have this to say: I am not a healer. I have no power to heal anyone. I am only a humble instrument in the hands of God, who does the work."

The healing line is indeed an interesting phase of the meeting. On occasions, I have sat where I could not see the evangelist, but could hear him clearly over the public-address system. I was surprisingly impressed with the interesting, running line of comment the evangelist carried on with those for whom he prayed. It goes something like this:

"Well, my Baptist sister, do you believe God will heal you tonight? Fine, I do too. Bless you! . . . Brother Blank, how are you? You flew down here from New York. Well, you certainly deserve help tonight. Go, and be made whole. . . . Let me have that child up here, please. My, what a beautiful little boy! Honey, do you know Jesus loves you? Well, He does and Brother Roberts is going to ask Jesus to heal you. . . . Sister, did you feel the power of God then? . . . Brother! You got something. Go on and believe God. . . . Brother, take that home with you!"

And on and on the comments go, while hundreds pour through the line. Now a tall, slender young man with sallow complexion stands before the evangelist's chair. Immediately a change comes over Oral

Roberts. His smile is gone. His face seems almost twisted in agony. One can easily picture what is going on in his mind. The young man is a TB patient, and Oral Roberts has in spirit slipped down into the sufferer's skin and is suffering with him. Once again, he is feeling the searing agony of his own days of dying with tuberculosis in both lungs. His shoulders twist convulsively, as if trying physically to throw off the clutch of the disease. Then he speaks, "My brother, I know what is wrong with you." Then, his face lifted heavenward, he prays, "Oh, God—the hot, searing pains, the lonely hours of suffering, the bed of torture!" And again a transformation takes place. He seems suddenly to realize that he is not the victim. He is the victor. His hand shoots out to the forehead of the TB sufferer, and in a voice vibrant with authority that even the devil must recognize, he demands: "Thou foul, tormenting TB, come out of this man! Come out of him! Come—on—out—of—him! Oh, glory! It's coming, Brother, did you feel that?"

Most of the time, the vast audience is well in hand. But a few times I have seen the people take over momentarily. Such a time was in the meeting already referred to. A little boy, accompanied by his mother, came hobbling up on crutches, one of his little feet securely bound in some kind of strap. Then the evangelist jumped out of his chair and came down with the child. He started praying for him, then suddenly looking up at the weeping mother, he asked, "Mother, do you want me to pray for you?" Tearfully, she nodded. Then he said, "I'm going to pray for you to get you out of the way. You have so much sympathy that you are not helping me a bit."

He prayed for the mother. Then he resumed his prayer for the child, and said, "Now, Son, you are going to walk off this platform without your crutches.

Let me see you walk." The child, with faith characteristic of his age, started walking without his crutches. Suddenly Brother Roberts cried, "Run, Son; run to your mother!" And the boy took him at his word and went running to his mother. Their joyful greetings over, the child was given his crutches which he placed on his little shoulder like a soldier carrying his rifle, and walked down the aisle for the thousands to see what God had done. The vast audience came to their feet with ecstatic rejoicing. The evangelist tried to bring them back to order, but for once they paid him no heed. Then, co-operating with the inevitable, he shouted, "Then help yourselves!" This time they took him at his word, and there was a high time in Zion that night.

I must tell you of one more instance. I sat on the platform looking back over the long line of sick people waiting for prayer, and I noticed a lady who seemed to be half carried, half dragged by two men, one holding onto each arm. I was particularly interested in this for some reason, and was glad when the cripple reached the evangelist's chair. He read her card and then commented: "What you really need is a restoration of all your muscles." She nodded assent. "That is going to require a miracle," he told her. "Actually, it is a little beyond my ministry of healing. But I am going to pray for you anyway. I am going to exercise all the faith I have, and I want you to believe with me." The woman agreed, and he started praying. Evidently he gathered help from his own prayer, for when it was finished, he left his chair and jumped to the lower platform where the woman was being helped up by the two men. "I am going to pray for you again," he told her. And he did so. "Now," he said, "you ought to be able to take some steps." And to one of the men he said, "Release her arm." And to the other, "Hold your hand lightly under her elbow. Let's see if she can take some steps." With this arrangement the woman took a few faltering steps. The evangelist radiated confidence. "I am going to pray for you once more," he said to the woman, "and you are going to walk off this platform alone." He kept his word. When the third prayer was ended, he instructed the man who was still holding her arm to turn it loose, and the woman walked off the platform unaided.

The story is endless, as endless as the lines of people who form to receive the benefits of Oral Roberts' prayers. To be perfectly honest one must admit that some go and apparently are not healed. Hundreds who seem to be healed afterwards suffer relapse. But forgetting the apparent failures, there are thousands who are still rejoicing in the day they first attended an Oral Roberts campaign. I personally know former cripples who are now walking normally, people who suffered with stomach trouble, heart ailments, nervous disorders and other maladies, who are now well. These are wonderful manifestations of God's power through His humble servant; but what is more wonderful is the vast multitudes of men and women who have found God precious to their souls. These will rise up in eternity to bless the man who showed them the way to God.

There were times, though, that the meetings did not go nearly so well such as in Amarillo, Texas, in 1950. On the last night of our crusade a tornado-like storm struck. The winds began to blow the big tent. I immediately told the people that as many as wished could go, but no one left his seat.

Then, while I was praying for the sick, there was a loud

clap of thunder and lightning hit nearby. Suddenly the lights went out. Seven thousand people including hundreds of babies and children were on the brink of disaster. The wind was whipping the tent and blowing with tornado-like force.

The big tent started up like a helium-filled balloon and then gently descended. The giant poles holding the canvas up began to fall toward the people.

As they started crawling out from the wreckage, hail was coming down fast and furious. The ground was wet and as they ran to their cars, many slipped and fell. There were many crippled, blind and seriously ill people. It was a major catastrophe.

I went around helping as much as I could. I found my own wife and small baby huddled under what was left of the platform. The next day the newspapers carried the story, MIRACLE IN AMARILLO. Only one person in seven thousand had to be hospitalized for any length of time and he was not injured seriously. Yet when I went out the next day to the crusade site, it was difficult to believe. Chairs were twisted, the tent in shreds, the lights and equipment destroyed, but no one had been killed and there was only one broken limb.

This disaster caused a temporary and involuntary closing down of my tent ministry. But it wasn't until 1967, almost seventeen years later, in Anaheim, California, that the big tent came down permanently and voluntarily, never to be put up again. The days of the big tent were over.

It was a hard decision to make, for when I purchased

my first tent and held my first tent meeting in Durham, North Carolina, in 1948 I was filled with excitement and enormous confidence at the way God would use this method. And it was effective. In those days few cities had an auditorium adequate for the crowds that attended our services. Those cities that did have large enough facilities had designed them for usage other than meetings of the type we held. The tent allowed us to have a place designed for specialized needs. Too, it attracted people who would never come to an auditorium or a church. There was an accessibility and informality that caused people of all stations of life to feel welcome.

Yet by the early sixties I could see that the tent was ceasing to be an asset. People were no longer attracted by its novelty. They had become used to cushioned chairs and air-conditioning and to watching television. Why go to our tent when they could watch our television program in the comfort of their own living room each week?

This declining trend began to be starkly clear both to me and my associates. But for a lot of people for me to leave the tent would be to leave the healing ministry. People see objects; they make methods sacred.

By 1968 I knew that not only were the tent crusades over in principle, they had to be over in fact. The decision was made in Anaheim and was never retracted.

Curiously, I have received many offers to buy the tent. One offer came from a group who wanted to sell small blocks of it as souvenirs. Other evangelistic ministers wanted to use it and take up where they felt I had left off.

Though the tent enabled us to reach thousands of people, the reason I could make such a change is because I've never married a method. I'm never bothered by changing methods. Whatever works best is what I want to use. The twenty years of the tent ministry were a unique experience and perhaps the last of its kind of that scale. It's an era that is over. But it became the nucleus for the beginning of a ministry that now reaches many times more . . .

CHAPTER 13

Reaching Out Through Television

By the early 1950s our crusades were creating national impact. Several magazines, such as *Life* and *Look*, carried stories on our ministry. Yet I had begun to feel restless. Though we had the largest tent in the world with packed services and positive results I was not satisfied. I felt God had called me to reach millions. The most crusades we could hold in a year were fourteen and these had to be limited to major population centers.

There were 26 million television sets in the United States and the number was growing every day. It was a new and exciting medium; people were captivated by TV and anxious to watch it.

I began working to use television as an outreach of my ministry. After several months of preparation and then working and filming in a studio, our first television program was premiered on January 10, 1954, over sixteen stations. The response was immediate. Overnight the number of people writing for prayer and our literature soared.

Yet there was something lacking. The programs had a woodenness about them that was stifling. I felt ineffective. I knew there had to be a better way.

During this period, Rex Humbard of Akron, Ohio, encouraged me to find a way to film directly in the tent. That was what I wanted too, but I didn't know how to get it done.

Eventually, we arranged for NBC to send a team from New York to one of our crusades and investigate the situation and make recommendations. Their professional analysis was very simple: "It can't be done." I had heard that before and I refused to accept it.

Finally, I located a film company who agreed to try it. The cost: $42,000! We didn't have that kind of money, but I asked them to come anyway. They said they would.

Now came the hard part. Where would we get $42,000? I began to study the Bible for a way to get at this problem. After much wrestling and praying, I felt I had it. I named it the Blessing Pact.

Then I called a meeting of those who were interested in seeing us go on television. At this meeting I shared with them several different instances from the Bible where people had been blessed by God for their giving. I said, "I am asking 420 people in this audience to pledge a hundred dollars each. I want you to let me enter into a Blessing Pact with you for one year. I will use your gift to win souls."

I then explained how I felt about giving. I told them that giving was like a seed you planted. They could and should expect something to happen when they gave. In this instance, their giving of one hundred dollars was a seed they were planting that would be used to win souls but because of their gift, they could expect a blessing in their own lives. I said, "I will earnestly pray that the Lord return your gift in its entirety from a totally unexpected source."

I then did something they were totally unprepared for. They had never been asked to give and then hear what I said—"I promise at the end of one year if God has not blessed you, I will return your money."

There was an audible gasp in the audience. The audacity of such a plan shook me a little, too. But I knew God had given me the plan and I felt it would open the doors of their minds to thinking and believing for bigger things in their own lives. Approximately 420 stood to accept the challenge.

(Two people later wrote for their money back. Naturally, I sent it. One of these then returned it and wrote, "I only wanted to see if you would keep your word.")

Now that the funds had been raised, there were other serious obstacles to hurdle. One of these was how the audiences in attendance at the crusades would respond to television. Big, bright, hot lights were to be stationed throughout. Cameras, recording devices, cables, crewmen were to be everywhere even though I knew some people would feel it sacrilegious to bring cameras into a worship service, and while I was extremely eager to get the filming done right, I was even more concerned that the filming might disturb the audience so that people would be less responsive to the invitation to be saved and to the releasing of their faith for healing.

My fears were groundless. There was a freedom in the service, and following my sermon, an unusual response of the unsaved. The same was true in the healing line. Dramatic healings were filmed for the first time in history, one right after another.

The first program filmed direct during the crusade was aired in February 1955. It created a national controversy. At our office in Tulsa we were flooded with calls, and television stations throughout North America were totally unprepared for the response they received. Their switchboards were jammed; their mail was unprecedented.

It shook some station managers so much that our program was canceled. Then they really began to get mail! Millions were excited by our program and wanted it shown on their favorite station.

One of the most widely publicized healings of my ministry occurred during those first programs. The healing of Anna Williams made the front page of nearly every major newspaper—Los Angeles, Chicago, Dallas, New York. A free-lance reporter went to Wichita Falls and wrote this story for our magazine:

In January 1951, Anna Williams had been involved in a train-car wreck. She sustained a severely fractured right leg and complications. Thrombophlebitis, a clotting of the blood, necessitated an operation before these clots could reach Anna's lungs. The clots finally dissolved, and Anna was released from Hermann Hospital, Houston, Texas—but on crutches.

By September 22, 1952, Anna had not yet abandoned her crutches when she was stricken with polio and rushed to Jefferson Davis Hospital, Houston's polio center. Polio had caused temporary, but nonetheless complete, paralysis, and there were many hours of pain and therapy in the days that followed. Two weeks later she was transferred to Hermann Hospital. The polio therapy was hampered because Anna was expecting their first child. Also, her old trouble, phlebitis, the blood condition that induced clots, re-activated making further polio therapy impossible. The baby, little Benjamin Rex, was born January 7, 1953. And on January 22, Anna was again released from Hermann Hospital—still on crutches.

A third crippling force entered into Anna's life—spondylitis, a disease similar to polio. This left her confined to a wheel chair.

On April 27, 1955, they moved to Wichita Falls, Texas, where her husband Bill, a sergeant in the Air Force, was to be stationed at Sheppard Air Force Base. Unable to find an apartment immediately, they moved in with some friends, Harold and Anna Weeks.

Mrs. Weeks had written Anna and Bill about the Oral Roberts television program and urged Anna then to watch it. But Anna was not able to see it where they lived. So Mrs. Weeks determined they should see it on the very first Sunday they were in her home.

Bill had suggested earlier that they attend the motorcycle races in Lawton, Oklahoma, but they found it so good to be home, they decided not to go. They sat happily relaxed in the Weeks living room as the Oral Roberts program came on. Anna sat comfortably on a divan where her husband had assisted her from her wheel chair. They listened spellbound to the sermon.

Then came the healing line. There was a little crippled boy, who was instantly healed by God's power. He strode triumphantly from the platform. Mrs. Weeks, watching for Anna's reaction, saw her catch her breath.

Oral Roberts then appeared on the screen in a close-up. He urged everyone in the TV audience to place his hand on his heart and pray either for himself or for others who needed healing.

Anna listened with both her mind and her heart as Brother Roberts prayed.

At this precise moment, the Holy Spirit entered into Anna's frail body and there was a general tingling throughout her entire being. Her legs felt strange and alive. An overpowering compulsion told her to GET UP AND WALK.

"Honey," she said, "help me get up." She reached out her hands. Bill was accustomed to helping his wife, so he walked over and took her hand. He had not caught the ecstatic look on Anna's face, and he was bewildered when she grasped his hands and pulled herself up from the divan under her own power.

Bill looked apprehensively at his wife. She was standing uncertainly, like a child who has not yet learned to walk. She lurched forward with staggering, unsteady steps. In panic, Bill grabbed for Anna's hand and attempted to steady her.

"Turn me loose!" she exclaimed. "I'm going to walk. God has hold of me."

Anna Williams did walk. Her steps may have been weak and unsteady at first, but she did walk.

Bill's eyes followed Anna with a look of combined concern and rejoicing. She walked the entire length of the living room and stopped at a table in the adjoining kitchen. She leaned against the table, tossed back her head and cried exultantly, "The Lord has healed me!"

The urge to praise God and the urge to continue walking were consuming her like fire. Again she walked that length of room, this time right into her husband's arms. Each step she took was just a trifle stronger, a little surer than the last. Again and again she exclaimed happily, "Look what God did!"

Anna could not stop walking. She picked up little Benny, raised him high over her head and laughed with the thrill of full motherhood. This was her child. Although he was 28 months old, this was the first time that she had ever had the strength to lift him. She swung Benny to the floor and sat playfully beside him. For the first time she could play with her baby on the floor. She sprang to her feet. Her joy was so complete that she flung herself about the room in happy, dancing movement.

After the newspapers had flashed the story of Anna's healing from coast to coast, Paul Harvey, the well-known ABC commentator, interviewed her the following Tuesday. Mr. Harvey had informed the people on his radio program that he would have a surprise guest at his lecture that evening at Midwestern University. And when the time came, he merely said, "Ladies and gentlemen, I would like you to meet a friend of mine: this is Mrs. Anna Williams." There was no further introduction, and none was needed, for by this time all Wichita Falls knew of the miracle on Eighth Street.

As Anna Williams walked up on the stage, you could have heard the proverbial pin drop. Anna walked like a slim, regal princess, proud of God's handiwork. She was not nervous. She felt no fear.

She hadn't planned her speech. She let God put the
words in her mouth. She told Paul Harvey's audience,
"If you believe and have faith, you will be healed."

Soon we were taking the ministry of the healing Christ
into the homes of millions with needs like Anna's. In
places where the only time available was 12:30 to 1:00
P.M. on Sundays, we actually had pastors write and complain that if they held over their services the least bit past
noon, people would leave so that they would be able to
see our program in its entirety. Our network blanketed
the continent. It gave a front-row seat in the crusades to
millions who might never have attended otherwise.

I was surprised to discover how many people watched
the program. When the team and I were received by the
late John F. Kennedy in the White House, he said, "Reverend Roberts, I've seen you on television and I enjoy it
very much."

The Reverend Warren Hultgrun, pastor of the First
Baptist Church in Tulsa, once introduced me at Rotary by
telling of a response to my programs he had heard. He
said, "I was in New York recently and rode in from the
airport in a cab. The driver was very talkative. He finally
asked me where I was from. When I said, 'Tulsa,' he almost lost control of the cab.

"'Let me ask you something,' he said. 'Every week my
old lady writes Oral Roberts for prayer. Sometimes she
sends a little money along. Tell me, is that guy on the
level?'

"I answered, 'I believe Oral Roberts to be a sincere
man of God who is doing great good in the world.'

"He said, 'Am I relieved to hear that! You know, I've been secretly watching him on TV myself!'"

At the time we went on television, my office staff in Tulsa numbered around 150 employees in a rather modest building. Since the first crusade in 1947, we had experienced a good solid growth. It started with Evelyn overseeing most of the work and three girls coming each evening to help her with the typing and office details. They used the garage in our house as office space. Then, as we began to grow, the whole house became office space and our family moved out. Finally we built a small office building, and later another larger one.

But after the first television show, we didn't just grow, we leaped. Soon our office employees numbered more than six hundred and space became critically scarce. Finally, in 1959, we dedicated the beautiful Abundant Life Building on the edge of downtown Tulsa. A seven-story white structure, it is still one of Tulsa's finest buildings.

By 1962 I began to feel restless again. Somehow the Lord has never let me be content with the status quo no matter how well others may think things are going. Our programs were being well received; interest in them continued to grow; but I felt disenchanted with their quality, for in the short life of television there had developed an amazing sophistication in programming. Viewers began to expect this in all the programs they saw. Though our programs were good, I felt they had not kept pace with the industry.

Then, too, as I watched them I began to detect an

overemphasis on my hands that was disconcerting, for it was an inaccurate representation of my ministry. To watch these programs, you got the feeling that my preaching, the reading of the holy scriptures, the prayers for the unsaved were all incidental to my hands being laid on the sick.

Many of the sermons were being filmed in studios now, though we still filmed the healing line direct from the crusades. I had gotten accustomed to television so that a studio no longer affected my preaching. But the formats had not really advanced and grown. They were still basically much like the very first ones. I met with the producers and directors, but although we discussed it at length, there was too strong a pattern already set in their minds. Little change came about.

I then sensed the inevitable. This phase of my ministry had peaked. Its effectiveness was declining. When I apprised my staff of this, they were horrified. They cited the statistics and the growth, but I was unimpressed.

Also, Oral Roberts University was in its birth stages, and I did not have time to get involved in a totally new television ministry. Instead, I began to effect cutbacks in the weak reception and response areas. If rates were increased sharply or if good time slots became unavailable, we dropped that station. Finally, in 1965, I made the decision to be off the air no later than the summer of 1967. One-half of the stations were dropped in 1966 and the remainder in May of 1967.

It was one of the hardest decisions I had to make, but it was necessary. I refused to marry any method and this one was now outdated. I knew my television ministry was not over, but I wanted enough interval to elapse so that when I came back I would not have to contend with an outdated method.

When we did return to the air in March of 1969, one of the persons who helped me develop a new thrust and format was my youngest son, Richard. But before this could happen he, like his older brother Ronnie, had to go through a period in which he would discover for himself what God wanted to do with his life.

Really it was not only Richard's problem, but mine and Evelyn's. Having problems with a son or daughter is certainly not unusual. I imagine you can count on your fingers the number of families in our country who don't have problems with their children, or children who don't have problems with their parents. It certainly comes to preachers' families as well.

When I became a minister, one of the scriptures that strongly influenced me was Luke 12:31, "Seek ye the kingdom of God; and all these things shall be added unto you."

I have tried to do that . . . to obey God's voice, to do what He has called me to do, to trust that He would take care of my family and that my children would become Christians and serve God.

In my ministry I have had to travel constantly throughout the world so it was really Evelyn who raised our four children. They didn't have much of a father from that standpoint. In the early days of my ministry I was at home only eight days a month. When I was home, I was with the children a lot, and I trained them in the Bible.

Many times I would give them a gift if they would memorize a verse or read a chapter in the Bible. I played with them. But yet I was away so much.

Sometimes I would ask Evelyn to go with me because as a husband, I would get lonesome, too, especially if I was overseas for several weeks at a time. We would have babysitters or friends come in and stay with the children. Sometimes it worked out well and sometimes it did not.

When we went to Australia in 1954, I asked Evelyn to go with me. I told her that I would be over there a long time and we could get someone to stay with the children. Richard was just a little boy at that time, and when we came home I went into his bedroom and someone had chopped off the bedpost. I said, "What happened?"

The lady who had stayed with him said, "Well, he was so upset that you were gone, and then he was more upset when his mother was gone, so he took his little hatchet and just cut off the bedpost!"

I remember when Richard was five years old we were in a crusade in Baltimore, Maryland. We stood him up on a chair before ten thousand people and he sang "I Believe." People were really touched and crying all over the audience. When we got home a neighbor of ours said, "How did you do, Richard?"

He replied, "I just brought the house down!"

As Richard grew up, his voice began to develop, and he began to sing for coffeehouses and to lean toward show business.

The more I wanted him to sing for me, the less he wanted to. One time especially I asked him to sing for me on a Sunday morning, and he said, "No, Dad. I don't want to sing for you."

It should not have hurt me, but it did. It really got down inside me. I began to understand the saying, "When they are little they step on your toes, but when they are older they step on your heart!"

When Richard graduated from high school he went to an out-of-state university. One day he came home. He said, "Dad, let's go out and play a game of golf." We went out on the golf course and he was hitting the ball a mile. He is a good golfer, but usually I could stay up with him. However, on this day I couldn't hit the ball because I was all bound up inside. I started trying to talk to him about his life and the concerns I had. And as we talked, I could see he was turning me off. I said, "Okay, let's just go."

So we picked up our clubs right in the middle of the game and went over to the car. And we sat there and just glared at each other. And I will remember it as long as I live. Finally, he said, "Dad, get off my back."

And then it came to me. Maybe I was on his back. Maybe I was trying to save him. I was not letting God do it. I thought about it a moment. I had prayed for him and all four children since they were babies. I had dedicated each of them to God. But now I had run out of prayers. So I said, "Okay, Richard, give me your hand."

With his hand in mine I said, "From this moment I am off your back. I am going to put you in the hands of God. And I will never mention God's name to you again unless you ask me."

I felt it had to be God's battle and not mine.

Richard went back to school and one day his mother received a phone call. He said, "Mother, I am tired of living in a dormitory. And if I were to come to ORU, would you let me stay at home?"

I had not mentioned to him anything about his going to ORU because I didn't think he would consider it even though I wanted him to go there with all my heart. His mother told him, "Certainly, Richard, but you have picked up some habits that we don't allow at ORU even if you are the president's son."

He said, "Mother, I can give those up."

She said, "Great. You can stay at home as long as you want to."

Of course both of us were thrilled and soon he had transferred to ORU as a sophomore. While he was there he met a young woman, Patti Holcombe, from Portland, Oregon. Patti was one of the finest singers we had on the campus. Richard began to develop a deep love for Patti. Soon he popped the question and a date for their marriage was set.

One day while I was away and Evelyn was at home by herself, the back door slammed and in walked Richard. Without any small talk he blurted out, "Mother, I am in trouble."

Evelyn said, "What's the trouble, Richard?"

He replied, "Something has happened to Patti. She can't get it through her head that I really love her. She is going to call the wedding off."

He kept on talking and soon the whole story was out. Patti was a dedicated Christian who wanted to use her life and talent for God. And she wanted to marry someone who had made the same commitment. As the wedding date got closer—one month away—the more she talked with Richard, the more she felt that Richard, even though he had become a Christian, was not at all committed to giving his life unreservedly to God.

So, despite the embarrassment, she was ready to give the ring back and to cancel all the wedding plans.

Finally, with his head in his mother's lap like when he was a little boy, they began to pray. Something really happened to Richard. For when they had finished praying he told his mother, "Everything's all right now. I don't want to give up Patti, but if that's the way it must be, okay. Regardless, I'm going to use my life for God." Then he picked up the phone and called me in California. When I answered he said, "Dad, everything is okay." I was a mighty happy father.

Later, Richard explained how he saw what had happened. "When I discovered that I hadn't really committed my life to the Lord the way I really should, I saw myself in a different light. It took almost losing what I wanted the most to make me turn around and say, 'God, I will do what you want me to do whether I keep Patti or not.'"

He said, "Now, instead of feeling you're always on my back, I think of myself at your side helping you in your ministry."

One day while I was on the West Coast I was scheduled to have lunch with Ralph Carmichael. Ralph is one of the outstanding conductors and arrangers in the music business. Many of his arrangements for stars like Nat King Cole, Roger Williams, and others have won critical acclaim from musicians and fans alike. Best of all, Ralph is a committed Christian. He had arranged the music for our radio programs for some time and had made an immeasurable contribution to our success.

On this particular day he invited Dick Ross, a friend of his, to lunch with us. Dick had been the founder and president of Worldwide Pictures and had produced and directed the majority of the motion pictures and television shows of the Billy Graham Evangelistic Association. He had left the Graham Association, however, and for some time had been working in the secular television industry where he had produced and directed several popular shows and specials.

But now he was anxious to do a totally new kind of religious television show. When he began to tell me of his dream, I knew I had found the right man.

Before long, Ralph, Dick, Richard, and I were involved in discovering what a new ministry would be like. I spent many hours in prayer. I listened a lot and kept open to new directions. The pieces began to fit together. I knew that because of my previous television ministry and being known throughout America as an evangelist, we could reach the church world. But that was not where the real need was. I felt led by God to try some daring new ways of proclaiming the Gospel.

The previous summer, the World Action Singers from ORU, had traveled in sixteen different countries overseas. They were a smash hit among old and young everywhere they went. They had a NOW sound. Richard had already begun to work with them, and I could see that their music would give us a distinctly new look.

Dick Ross and Ralph Carmichael had many excellent contacts in the entertainment world. Ralph had arranged music for the biggest singers in the business. Dick and his staff had produced several successful shows and had the respect of many of the best-known stars in the business.

To get the unchurched to watch us, we would have to have name stars. Our program would have to be in prime time, and it would have to have the look and musical sound of top-flight productions. We were aiming for the people in need across the land who did not know Christ.

Finally the pattern emerged. We would tape weekly shows at ORU for viewing on Sunday mornings. But our main thrust would be quarterly prime time specials which would be taped at NBC studios in Burbank, California. These specials would have famous guests, special sets and wardrobes, new music—the works.

Then, I ran into a snag. Traditionally, when religious music is sung, it is performed by church choirs in robes and in choir lofts. The choir members stand as still as wooden Indians. Movement and feeling are forbidden.

When we began to discuss the music and the World Action Singers, Richard immediately began to protest the old pattern of the choir. "Dad, if you're going to reach young people, that won't work. Young people feel their music. We have to move and express what is going on inside."

We talked about it for a long time. I knew he was right and yet I knew how hard it is to break down old ideas and customs. After a while I decided that if we were going to reach the unchurched, we would have to be willing to risk something new; we couldn't let ourselves be ruled by outdated and irrelevant ideas of procedure. We hired one of television's best choreographers.

Because of the racial conflict in the nation at that time, I was moved to deal with this issue on my first special. God gave me a sermon entitled "Touching People." So that we would have the blacks listening I very much wanted to have a black star. My first choice was Miss Mahalia Jackson. Mahalia had been a warm friend of mine for years. Fortunately, she was not booked at the time of our taping and consented to appear.

Soon we were ready. We had agreed to do one show as a pilot. If there was a good response from the television industry, we would proceed with others. Taping was scheduled for the Christmas holidays so the World Action Singers would not miss classes at ORU.

As a warm-up, Richard and the Singers appeared on the Joey Bishop Show and were a smash hit. We then went into rehearsals for the "Oral Roberts Contact Special." Soon we were ready. Our announcer was from "Bonanza," the technical crew from "Laugh-In," with a set built by NBC. The cameras rolled, the music sounded, the announcer began.

A live audience was present. They cooperated beautifully during retakes. After several hours we were through. I felt we had it. Richard's music brought raves from Mahalia and others around the set. The Singers were outstanding. And, of course, Mahalia touched the people with her own unique way of singing the Gospel.

I had felt unusual freedom while preaching. It was easy to zero in on one person, to see one man in need and talk to him.

Now came the test. What would be the television industry's reaction? Would they see this as bona fide prime-time programming or would we be pushed into bad time slots and given the low viewing hours?

I knew the competition among the networks as well as the local stations in the various cities was very keen. They would not sell time at any price to a program that their listeners would not watch.

But before long, the representatives were calling in excitedly. They were having great response. Most station managers were dubious, but once they saw the tape they changed their mind. And we felt that even those stations which turned us down could soon be won.

Immediately, plans began for the first special to be aired in March 1969. It was shown in every state of the Union and the provinces of Canada. It created a sensation in the religious field. For a religious group to use the medium of television creatively was a new experience. We had taken Jesus' commandment to go into all the world seriously. We had entered the world of secular entertainment and made it serve as a way of getting the attention of the unchurched. The first half of the show got their attention and then kept them with us in the second half as we shared the message God had given us. I always concluded with a prayer for the needs of the people.

The mail response was one of the heaviest of my ministry. People who had never written before asked for prayer and expressed their support for this type of effort. We knew now that we were in the right stream. This was the new way God had directed our television ministry.

Plans then began for other specials with stars like Pat Boone, Anita Bryant, Dale Evans, Jerry Lewis, Jimmy

Durante, Lou Rawls, Kay Starr, Sarah Vaughn, and Jimmy Rogers. We taped a Christmas Show, specials for youth, Easter, Thanksgiving, Valentine's Day. We even went to Japan and taped a special at EXPO '70.

Though a few traditional church people misunderstood some of the shows, I had to measure our effectiveness by the results. And it was clear that more people were hearing the Gospel through this ministry than ever before (our Thanksgiving Special had over 27 million viewers). Also, more people in need had written requesting my prayers than at any time before. Testimonies of people helped and healed, of homes put back together, lives changed and new directions gained had been sent in by the thousands.

And something else happened that I had never experienced before: thousands of young people tuned in. They wrote for advice, guidance, and prayer. Because of this development, my son Richard began assuming a larger role and share of the responsibility. God continues to use him in a marvelous way.

I'm not committed to this method forever. When the tent was no longer effective, we quit using it. When my old TV programs were no longer reaching as many as they should, we dropped them. But I'm convinced that television is one of the most effective and exciting ways to reach people where they are. We intend to continue making large use of it.

CHAPTER 14

Oral Roberts University

Recently, Senator Mark Hatfield spoke at Oral Roberts University in Tulsa. During his address he mentioned a visit I had had with him in Portland, Oregon, in the early 1960s while he was still governor. At that time ORU was more a dream than a reality. Limited building had begun, architectural designs were under way, publicity and brochures were just coming off the press.

Naturally, when he dropped by the hotel, I was eager to get his response because he had himself been an educator before entering politics.

Fortunately, though, on that day he didn't give me his real opinion. It wasn't until ten years later that he told the student body what it really was:

A number of years ago Oral Roberts was in Portland, Oregon. Through some folders and papers he had he wanted to show me of a dream of his. And in the Sheraton-Hilton Hotel in Portland he unfolded these pictures of his concept of a university. I remember looking at him and I saw the intent vision in his eye. I thought to myself, "Oral, you are a man of great vision, but, oh, you are so visionary." And I must say that I was a man of no faith. When I come here today and see the realization of this vision, of this dream, I see that it's more than Oral Roberts. It's evidence of how God can work through a man.

It's told among our office staff in Tulsa that when I announced in late 1961 we were going to build a university, one office wag said, "It will never happen."

Then he paused and said, "By the way, where do I enroll?"

On a 180-acre tract that grew to 500 acres in south Tulsa, Oklahoma, the great earth-moving machines started clearing the ground in early 1962. At the same time the building program started, the search was initiated for faculty and administrators. And all the while, on every side, we were being told that it couldn't be done.

A campus couldn't be built. A Board of Regents could not be assembled. Qualified instructors and administrators would never come. An adequate library was impossible to acquire that quickly. Students wouldn't enroll. State accreditation would not be given, and certainly regional accreditation would never be granted.

But they were wrong on all counts. On March 31, 1971, ten years after we broke ground and six years after we opened the first class, every one of these impossibilities had been achieved.

Our physical plant was evaluated at over 30 million dollars. Student enrollment was more than 1,000 with young people from 49 states and 23 foreign countries. The faculty numbered 78. Library volumes totaled 121,000. Audio-visual aids numbered 30,000. A strong Board of Regents from across America and Canada was actively functioning. Both state and regional accreditation had been given.

It had not been easy. Nothing worthwhile ever is.

The greatest initial obstacle was getting the funds to build the buildings. As in most things, I kept praying to find a solution. Finally, God let me know that I should start with the same thing He used when He made the universe—NOTHING!

And that's what we did. I announced we were going to build even though we had nothing to build with. From "nothing" there was no way to go but up. Scores said it would be impossible. I refused to accept that. Because of my faith in God, I was unwilling to believe that anything was impossible. My whole life had been a series of overcoming impossible situations.

When I was a backward, stammering boy, I overheard my uncle tell my father, "That boy will never amount to a hill of beans."

At age seventeen with tuberculosis in both lungs, my friends discussed in hushed tones how long it would be before my death.

In 1947 I was advised to keep my little church and stay in the pastorate if I wanted to have any future at all as a minister.

By 1962, I had faced bullets, mobs, stink bombs, tornadoes, fire, hatred, libel, character assassination and need in every form. But we had only grown stronger.

One distinct advantage I had in building a new university was that I didn't know the problems involved. All I knew was that I felt God wanted me to build it. I went at it with the same single-mindedness as any of the tasks which He had called me to accomplish.

The first three buildings were completed and ready for interim use by January 1963. We began holding seminars for clergy and laymen, youth seminars for potential students and even an International Seminar with delegates from over fifty different countries.

Finally, in the fall of 1965, the doors opened for the first class with three hundred bright young freshmen from all over America, Canada, and several foreign countries. The faculty had been painstakingly selected. Over one-half of them held earned doctorates.

It was an exciting and rewarding beginning. At the opening banquet, I made this challenge to the students:

> Wholesomeness will be a way of life here. Here you can reach for excellence and find it. If your muscles are flabby, you will have to toughen them. If you have been sheltered, you will have to make adjustments to the outside world. Competition is furious out there. To make the grade, you will have to call forth every resource of your inner and outer man—in short, you will have to stand up on the inside and be able to take the offensive. . . .
>
> I am asking you to get the vision of wholeness . . . and to help start a unique trend toward sanity and achievement in this exploding civilization.

A fundamental reason for your being here is that you want to engage your mind in an earnest study of your world, a discipline of genuine inquiry, in learning to think and reason, and in making something of yourself that will benefit mankind. . . .

In a world which no longer seems to place a high priority on self-discipline, it is well to keep in mind Thomas Huxley's statement:

"Perhaps the most valuable result of all education is the ability to make yourself do the thing you have to do, when it ought to be done, whether you like it or not; it is the first lesson that ought to be learned."

To develop your intellect fully learn the art of asking questions. Throughout His lifetime, Jesus probed, questioned, reasoned and sought answers wherever there was something to be learned; to be done; to be changed. He never accepted the status quo. He always believed there was something more, an even greater revelation. He wanted men to be free in thought and to keep the inquiring mind always. He placed no limit on the revelation of truth and none shall be placed on it here. . . .

Hear this, and hear it well. You are not here to "goof off." We know that you realize that life is too exciting, your potential too promising, and your opportunities on this campus too unlimited to waste your time and ours. . . . Analyze, crystallize, come to important new conclusions. Be willing to change when new information moves in.

It is our earnest desire and purpose to make ORU not only tops academically, but a foremost university in the formation of character. Character is spiritual and moral fiber of vigor especially instilled by self-discipline and commitment to principle. This, of course, rules out cheating in every form because cheating cheapens your character. Let me emphasize

that while we are innovators in educational techniques, we are definitely old-fashioned when it
comes to Christian morals. We respect the integrity
of each student and you will want to earn that respect.

Admittedly this is a difficult area in which to work.
It is not fashionable to teach college students to develop their spiritual life. They go forth into society
as "angry young men," rich in intellect and knowl-
edge, but poor indeed in spirit. This is one of the
reasons America today bears all the earmarks of
spiritual decline and moral decay, and is, as Toynbee
has said, in the "ebbtide of civilization."

The world doesn't need more college students to
wave flags, carry placards, halt traffic, and riot
against law and order. What our civilization needs is
for you to make your spiritual development a normal
part of your education. I pray through this development you will build your life pattern.

That was in 1965, and it was an exciting year. Naturally,
there were some adjustments and changes that had to be
made. Some students dropped out; a few had to be sent
home. But the overwhelming majority of this class realized the uniqueness of their being first. They responded
excitedly.

By 1967, enrollment had doubled. There were now
seven major buildings on a five-hundred-acre campus.
We had received national acclaim for innovation and
creativeness. The Ford Foundation called the Learning
Resources Center "one of the most creative facilities on
the American campus today."

In the center of the campus the Prayer Tower was
erected, the symbol of this ministry's presence on campus.

It housed the Abundant Life Prayer Group, a twenty-four-hour prayer counseling service, the chaplain's office, and an FM radio station. It also served as the focal point for campus tours and information.

Finally, on April 2, 1967, we were ready for the dedication of the University and my investiture as president.

Twenty thousand people from all over America and Canada attended. These included many of my lifelong partners and friends as well as distinguished educators, congressmen, senators, the governor, the mayor, and a large delegation of religious officials.

The Reverend Dr. Billy Graham was the dedicatory speaker. It was a typical, windy Oklahoma day. Billy asked me, "Oral, does the wind always blow this hard in Oklahoma?"

I answered, "Why no, Billy. Sometimes it blows harder."

Billy made an immeasurable contribution that day. With his bronzed face, his academic robe flapping with each gust of the Oklahoma wind, his jaw set with determination, and his finger pointing to stress each word, Billy took on the image of a prophet of old. And like a prophet, he delivered a charge to the people that brought them to an immediate awareness of their responsibility in this hour of destiny and dedication:

> This institution was built by the prayers, the dedication and money of men and women who love God, who believe the Gospel and who believe the Bible is the Word of God.
> If ORU ever moves away from faith in God and

putting God first, then let us this day pronounce a curse on it.

Let the regents, the faculty and the students be sure that they understand the purposes and the objectives of ORU. Many a school that was forged in the flames, exists today only in smoke. May ORU produce a holy enthusiasm for the will of God.

I propose that you determine this day to keep a personal relationship between faculty and students. Secondly, I propose that you determine this day to keep the faith of those who founded this institution. Thirdly, I propose that you determine this day to develop strong minds and bodies and high moral standards. Fourthly, I propose that you determine this day to keep an emphasis on evangelism.

To this end we dedicate ORU.

It was a humbling experience for me. My own education had been interrupted in high school by devastating illness. It was only after I was married and had a family that I was able to complete high school and enter college.

Now, as I addressed the thousands who had come, I told them what I felt our reason for being really was:

We believe that God is not yet done with man. This is the reason for the birth and dedication of one of America's newest private Christian universities. ORU was raised up by God through its trustees and regents to become part of the answer instead of part of the problem.

When our first graduates leave ORU they will not really be leaving the University. They will be taking with them the dream, the concepts, the answer of which they have become so much a part. They will take it out into the world, into the arena of man's desperate need, and reproduce that which they have become. Through the lives of its graduates, ORU will be more than a charismatic academic institution nestled in the lovely hills of Tulsa, Oklahoma. It will become a dynamic way of life at the base of human need in every area of man's activity throughout the world.

When the dedication day was over, I felt its success was a symbol from God that we were going to make it.

The greatest hurdle ahead of us now was accreditation. State accreditation had come quite early; regional accreditation was another matter.

We were told that the North Central Association of Colleges and Seconday Schools did not usually consider a school eligible for accreditation until three, full, four-year graduating classes had finished. Even then, we would probably be granted only provisional three-year status. Many schools we discovered had stayed on provisional accreditation from nine to twelve years, and even as long as twenty years. As we analyzed the situation, it looked as though we were facing a ten- to twelve-year project. But that did not satisfy me. I knew we could do it if we had the faith, initiative, and would work at the job, setting goals of excellence and refusing to settle for less.

The dean of academic affairs at that time, and chief mover of the accreditation effort, was Dr. John D. Messick. Dr. Messick had a distinguished educational background and had only recently retired as president of East Carolina State College in North Carolina.

One thing that especially recommended him was the

fact that he had served as an examiner for the regional accrediting association in the South, in addition to being a member of the board of directors.

Because of my inexperience, I left the matter of accreditation almost exclusively in his hands. He fashioned an exciting academic program and was instrumental in the selection of a quality faculty.

But his major assignment was to prepare us for regional accreditation at the earliest possible date.

The initial step was submission of a self-study document in May of 1966. The first class was wrapping up its opening year. This self-study discussed ORU's task as an institution and the resources (faculty, finances, library, physical plant) available to carry out the task. The study discussed whether the programs of the University were adequate to carry out that task, the level of faculty morale, the relevance of the students' life on campus to the task envisioned, and levels of student achievement.

A North Central evaluation team visited ORU in the fall of 1966. ORU had requested "candidate status." Dr. Messick and I went to Chicago in March 1967 to learn their decision. The meeting was peremptory and unsettling. We were turned down. Instead, we were given the new introductory rank created that year of "correspondent status." I was disappointed but not discouraged. We returned to Tulsa and went back to work.

Part of the planning with Dr. Messick had been that as we approached accreditation, a successor to him would be selected to carry on the program.

Shortly before going to Chicago, Dr. Messick and I had settled on a young English professor from the faculty, Dr. Carl H. Hamilton.

Carl was only thirty-three and had at one time served as editor of *Abundant Life* magazine at the Evangelistic Association. He knew what this ministry meant to people in a very personal way. At one time his own little girl had been near death and in need of healing.

It started mildly enough. His one-year-old daughter, Carla Jo, contracted chicken pox. They thought of it as nothing more than a childhood disease until, by the time the chicken pox should have been over, Carla Jo was getting worse. She was soon running a high fever. By Saturday afternoon she could not eat or drink.

Sunday morning her condition worsened to the point that she had to be hospitalized. The doctor made his diagnosis—the most extensive cellulitis (a form of blood poisoning) he had seen in his practice, and dehydration. The only hope he gave was, "We will do all we can to save her."

On Monday, the pediatrician gave the results of his further examination. "I don't want to frighten you, but because of the stiffness in her neck, I believe that the strep infection has penetrated the spinal column causing meningitis. We will do a spinal tap immediately to find out for sure."

When he said this, Carl's wife Joyce could hardly control her sobs of grief. She had worked in a medical office for nine years and when the doctor left, she turned to Carl and said, "Honey, the doctor is just trying to condition us for what he thinks is inevitable. He believes Carla Jo is going to die!"

On Tuesday afternoon Carl called my home. I was out, but he told Evelyn what had happened. She promised

him she would get in touch with me. Within thirty
minutes I was at the hospital.

Due to the serious nature of the illness, the nurses insisted that I put on a surgeon's mask and gown. They
were explicit in their instructions that I could only go in
the room and stand by the baby and pray—I could not
under any circumstances lay my hands on her.

When I entered the room, Carla Jo was lying listlessly
under an oxygen tent with an intravenous feeding tube
in her arm. My heart went out to her. I wanted to touch
her, to pray for her, to believe for God's healing power.
But she was completely encased and to make sure she
remained that way, a nurse was on the opposite side
watching my every move.

But while I stood there, incredible as it may seem, Carla
Jo began to work one of her little feet through an opening in the oxygen tent. As her little foot stuck out I
touched it briefly and said a short prayer, turned and left.

When Joyce returned to the room, for the first time the
baby was alert. She recognized her mother and had her
feet high in the air examining the sheet that was covering
her. Carla Jo's respiration rate gradually began to return
to normal and her kidneys began to function. The nurses
and doctors could not understand the improvement in
her condition. There was no medical reason for the sud-
den change.

From that point on, every day was a better day. Her
condition steadily, unwaveringly improved. By Thursday
morning her lungs were completely free of pneumonia
and she was taken out of isolation.

Two days after her first birthday, after sixteen days of

hospitalization, Carla Jo was released from the hospital.

A couple of years ago when Carla Jo was nine she came on our television program with her mother and dad. You never saw a healthier girl in your life. When I asked her who healed her, she said, "Jesus healed me!" and her beautiful brown eyes sparkled.

When ORU was founded, Carl had asked for a leave of absence from the association to complete his graduate work. When he had only his doctoral dissertation to complete, he applied to teach at ORU. Naturally, he was accepted and was doing an outstanding job. I recognized in him a combination of background, interest, experience, and training that was unique among the entire faculty.

Dr. Messick agreed. Carl was recommended for the post of associate dean of academic affairs, and the Board of Regents approved.

Now, though, we were in a new ball game. Dr. Messick was in his seventies, we had been turned down in our first accreditation effort, and it looked as if the burden of carrying the program would rest on an inexperienced administrator who would be one of the youngest deans in the country.

Dr. Messick had been persuaded in 1963 to come to ORU for five years. He still had his home in North Carolina. He had performed a job which no other man was capable of. Now it was time for him to leave.

Carl took over as dean of academic affairs in February 1968. Because of his inexperience, it meant I would also have to assume more responsibility than before.

Would we make it?

At Chicago I kept feeling that the committee was concerned in great part with the role I was playing. Healing through faith in God was anathema to many educators. The fact that ORU had the name of one synonymous with healing by faith was no small hurdle.

There had been many pressures to de-emphasize the spiritual commitment of ORU. Several had suggested that we didn't need to find faculty who were committed to the motifs of my ministry. But I knew that kind of compromise would result in losing the very thing for which God had raised up ORU. I knew whatever you compromised to get, you would ultimately lose. I wanted to live by the law of faith.

A second self-study was submitted. This time we were granted "candidate" status in March 1969. A third self-study, asking for three-year provisional status, was submitted in May 1970. Another evaluation team visited the campus in November 1970.

We were examined from our hair to our toenails. Any dissatisfied faculty member was queried long and hard to try and find any evidence of lack of academic freedom. Students were interviewed as well as regents.

During this time, one faculty member's contract was not renewed because of questions concerning his teaching competence. The chairman of his department recommended that he not be rehired. Dr. Hamilton concurred and I accepted their decision.

The man in question was incensed. He wrote the Board of Regents, organized student protests, and when this failed, he decided to try and really hurt us. Naturally, because of his faculty involvement in the self-study, he was aware of the critical nature of our status at that time.

The whole area of academic freedom was so sensitive that if he could prove he was fired because of administrative reaction to his teaching views, we would be in trouble.

He sent a letter to North Central charging us with suppression of academic freedom. We were asked to respond to the charges. We knew this was a serious matter. If it could be shown that indeed there was not academic freedom at ORU, our chances for accreditation would be nil. On the other hand, if it could be demonstrated that we had handled this situation in keeping with the best professional ethics, and that there had been just cause, it would be a blessing in disguise. The evaluation team would have one of the best examples possible for examining our institutional self-understanding.

Carl then prepared a dossier. Minutes were on file which showed that the request not to rehire the man originated with his departmental chairman. Memoranda were available from Carl to me citing the reasons for his concurrence. When the man had protested, an appropriate faculty committee of his peers had also met and rendered the same verdict. Carl then obtained letters from other institutions with which the man had worked before he came with us. Each of these stated that they had experienced similar problems with him.

When the facts were assembled by the evaluation team, they commended us for the manner in which the matter had been handled. Our commitment to quality education had been tested and vindicated.

Since accreditation also is based on the ability of the school to stay open and keep functioning, the evaluation team was concerned that after my death the school might have to be closed. The endowment fund and financial systems were given an extensive examination.

Finally, on March 29, 1971, I went before the executive committee in Chicago. Most of these men had never been to the campus and had never met me. I didn't know what to expect. They had the final say: yes or no. Carl Hamilton accompanied me. The committee was both courteous and curious. Their questions indicated genuine interest, but they gave no hint as to their decision. Would we make it? There was no way of knowing. The committee's final recommendation would be given by noon, Wednesday, March 31.

It seemed to me that was a long time to wait. I went back to Tulsa, and Carl stayed to learn their decision. He was to call me immediately when he found out. The hours passed unbearably slowly. Finally, at 9:45 A.M. Wednesday, the phone rang.

He started to explain the decision. I stopped him. "Carl, did we get it or not?"

He said, "Oral, they did something totally unheard of. Instead of giving us three-year provisional accreditation, we were given full and complete accreditation. There are no more applications and examinations for ten years."

Now instead of waiting another ten to twelve years, we had received accreditation in less than six years from the time classes had opened.

Carl called less than fifteen minutes before chapel was to begin. Everybody in the school had been on pins and needles to hear what the decision was. I walked into the chapel without any overt display. When I was introduced, I told them of the struggle we had gone through since

1961. I explained how important accreditation was. Then I listed the options: continue on candidate status, receive three-year provisional accreditation, or be rejected completely.

I told them we had not gotten any of these. They were floored. Instead we had been granted something better: complete and full accreditation.

When it hit them bedlam broke loose. Before I knew what had happened, the students had me on their shoulders like a coach at the basketball game. Needless to say, school came to a screeching halt.

Many of these students had turned down scholarships from prestigious schools to attend ORU. Our athletes had come knowing that if we were not accredited, they would never be able to play in major NCAA competition including post-season tournaments. They had risked these things to participate in an impossible dream. Now that dream had come true.

Likewise, the faculty were exuberant. Some of them had left outstanding colleges and universities to join us. Some of them had held departmental positions, had faculty tenure and higher pay. They risked their careers to become a part of the same impossible dream.

For the first time ever, we gave a holiday for the rest of the week.

Both the Tulsa newspapers carried big news articles. Then on their editorial page they analyzed why it was important:

> Something good happened to Oral Roberts Wednesday. In a precedent-shattering action the

North Central Association of Colleges and Secondary Schools announced that Oral Roberts University
is being granted full accreditation after less than six
years of existence.

Any suspicion that its founder was trying to puff
a Bible college up into a university has long since
vanished. ORU's determination to be excellent in
learning is now obvious, and the physical plant is one
of the leading tourist attractions in Tulsa.

But there's something more yet—the ORU atmosphere. The kids who leap forward to hold the door
open for you. The smiles. The unashamed prayers.
The aura of decency and good humor. Maybe these,
too, have something to do with a university's ability
to make a contribution to its times.

Beyond this there is the matter of grace—the kind
of grace in which a man contributes to the quality
of life.

We like to think that there is this grace at ORU
that in some happier time will be fashionable in this
great nation.

That makes the accreditation of ORU doubly welcome.

—Tulsa *Tribune*, April 2, 1971

The Tulsa *World*'s editorial added an interesting
comment:

. . . It also will make some new believers for
Roberts himself. When he talks now about bringing
a national basketball championship to Tulsa in a few
years, it sounds far-fetched and ever presumptuous
—but those who are quick to snicker should know
that he is a specialist at making scoffers eat their
words.

—Tulsa *World*, April 2, 1971

It was the greatest day in ORU's short, short history. We had our base. Now we were ready to launch our greatest venture of faith—to send a new kind of student into the world.

One of the questions often asked is what kind of exposure to my healing ministry are students given. Several people have speculated on it. And in a humorous vein one newspaper columnist wrote that there were no written examinations at ORU, only "oral" ones. Another said that there was a class offered each semester in "oral" interpretation.

Though there have never been specific courses on my ministry, the great majority of our students do embody the motifs and concerns of my twenty-five years as an evangelist. The spirit of the ministry is there. Praying for a sick friend is as common to them as taking the same friend to the doctor. Speaking in tongues and the manifestations of the gifts of the Holy Spirit are not esoteric, abnormal activities but natural expressions of committed Christian living. Going to people at the point of their need is something the faculty and students do as naturally as they breathe.

Excellence is expected in all areas—intellectually, spiritually, and physically. Even in athletics. The world of sports is one of the greatest opportunities to witness a Christian has. Our basketball team, the ORU Titans, has never had a losing season; they are shooting for the national crown. I expect them to make it—and soon!

We are striving for ORU to be big enough to meet the needs of its students, but small enough to know each one by his name; to be rigorous enough academically to challenge the most earnest scholar, but spiritual enough to draw him to his knees in worship and praise to God; to be competitive enough in athletics to win championships, reverent enough for each athlete to be a witness for Christ; to be strong enough in faith to expect a miracle.

I have no doubt whatever that ORU students will always seek to be involved in efforts to solve the staggering problems of mankind—whether it is sickness, hunger, ignorance, prejudice, war, misuse of the environment, or any of the multitude of problems confronting our world. ORU seeks to produce students committed to meeting needs.

Before classes opened at ORU I was visiting with a young Ph.D. who later joined our faculty. He said, "Dr. Roberts, what will happen to your ministry when you die? Will you have someone to fill your shoes?"

I assured him that was a very good question. Then I asked him if he had any thoughts on it. He answered, "Success without a successor is failure. ORU is the true successor of your ministry to people in need."

Later as I reflected on this, I began to see the day when thousands of highly trained young men and women would graduate and enter into the business and professional world. They would be equipped to reproduce this ministry in the marketplace—in the arena of human need. It is an exciting feeling. Through our students, whether they are in business, the professions or ministers of the Gospel, this ministry will go on.